A
DEFENSE
THAT
DEFENDS

Blocking Nuclear Attack

Lt. Gen. Daniel O. Graham, USA (Ret.)
and
Gregory A. Fossedal

INTRODUCTION BY RICHARD V. ALLEN

DEVIN-ADAIR, PUBLISHERS
Old Greenwich, Connecticut

Some material contained in the text has previously appeared in *The Wall Street Journal, Policy Review, Conservative Digest, The Washington Times, The Dartmouth Review, Public Research Syndicated,* and *Human Events.* Reprinted by permission.

Library of Congress Cataloging in Publication Data

Graham, Daniel Orrin, 1925-
  A defense that defends.

  Includes bibliographical references and index.
  1. United States—Air defenses, Military.
2. United States—Military policy.   3. Atomic warfare.
4. Astronautics, Military—United States.
5. Directed-energy weapons.   I. Fossedal, Gregory A.
II. Title.
UG733.G7   1983   355'.0335'73   83-10121
ISBN 0-8159-5317-8

DEDICATED

To Ronald Reagan, who had the courage to start this nation on the road to a true defense.

—Daniel O. Graham

To Donald Elmer Fossedal and *The Dartmouth Review,* sources of joy and inspiration.

—Gregory A. Fossedal

Devin-Adair, Publishers, is America's foremost publisher of quality conservative books. Founded in 1911, the company has championed the cause of the Thinking Right, and historically has published the work of major conservative writers. In recent years, Devin-Adair has increased its emphasis in this area and today is considered the leading publishing firm of the right.

The firm also has a long-standing reputation for works of significance in the fields of ecology, Irish literature, health, and nutrition. It publishes superbly illustrated nature and travel books on the Eastern seaboard through its Chatham Press subsidiary.

Devin-Adair's newest emphasis is in the area of books, programs, and software relating to the personal computer.

Devin-Adair operates the Veritas Book Club for conservative readers, the Ecological Book Club for nature and health audiences, and the Irish-American Book Society.

Publisher: C. de la Belle Issue
Managing Director: Roger H. Lourie
Cover Design: Gregory V. Clow
Book Design & Production: Arthur Hamparian
Typesetting: Coghill Book Typesetting
Printed at R. R. Donnelley & Sons

Devin-Adair, Publishers
P.O. Box A
Old Greenwich, Connecticut 06870

EXCELLENCE, SINCE 1911

Contents

Introduction

Books offering vital, fundamental and truly revolutionary ideas are seldom accepted at face value, and are often disregarded by those who rule the world of books. But here we deal with a book that quite literally deserves our undivided attention, because it addresses the question of the nation's survival, and shows how—in the opinion of the authors—we can reverse the relentless pressures to rely solely on weapons of mass destruction.

This book is a threat to conventional wisdom because it is a book that urges us to adopt a policy of *strategic defense,* a policy that will result in an actual shield against nuclear attack. This notion has been embraced by President Reagan, and that alone is enough reason for arresting our attention.

Strategic defense is not a new idea, but rather an idea whose time has come. Quite naturally, it has its detractors, and among them many distinguished specialists with outstanding credentials. But the annals of military history are replete with examples of new ideas, inventories and technologies spurned by the experts and practitioners of the day; and often those who assailed those innovations learned, through disappointment and bitter experience, that their opposition to new concepts was in fact unwise, and in some cases even retarded the objective of providing security.

That said, I do not agree with everything in this book, but I do know that we now have available a comprehensive analysis of the strategy, economics, technology and politics of defending the U.S. and its allies from nuclear war. If the authors do not manage to answer every conceivable question that I and others will have about strategic defense, the central thesis cannot be declared invalid. We are challenged by their provocative, yet compelling presentation of their case.

Those who are not familiar with the strategic defense concept are in for a rare and absorbing treat. The case for such a defense, which is simply a revolution in nuclear strategy, is laid out in a clear and understandable way, leaving no one behind. Still, it may upset the layman to contemplate the fact that for more than twenty years, the United States has consciously avoided—not just missed or overlooked, but deliberately, thoughtfully, carefully, purposefully avoided—almost any suggestion of protecting American citizens from Soviet nuclear weapons, once launched. There has been a generation of debate on this crucial issue, and the principal architects of our defense strategy have traditionally insisted that we forsake active defense because it is "destabilizing" and could be construed by the Soviets as "provocative." The dominance of this way of thinking has resulted in a reduction in our nation's security.

Our condition of defenselessness was emphasized in March 1983, when President Reagan delivered a nationwide address announcing that the future direction of our defense policy ought to be one of harnessing our technology and our ingenuity to develop effective defenses against Soviet weapons of mass destruction.

Some commentators wasted no time in attacking the President's revolutionary proposal; others were horrified at the suggestion the United States should find ways to *defend* itself, arguing that such a shift in U.S. strategy would "intensify" the arms race and "force" the Soviets to follow our lead; and still others dismissed the proposals as a tactical ploy designed to shield the Administration against the political challenge posed by the growing nuclear freeze movement and spreading opposition to the MX missile.

Those acquainted with General Daniel Graham and his work knew otherwise. Graham's initiatives, with which I have been familiar since their inception, received an important boost in 1981 when The Heritage Foundation decided to provide support for his proposal to perform hard, technical research on the prospects for strategic defense. This distinguished, dedicated personal friend and military man, it turned out, had always questioned why the United States had concentrated all its efforts on offensive weapons and hardly at all on defense. By 1982, Graham and a group of scientists, engineers and economists produced a detailed technical report outlining just how workable the concept could be. Their works clearly influenced the President, who incorporated much of it in his March 1983 speech.

Sometime after issuing the report, and before the President's speech, Graham encountered Gregory Fossedal, a journalist who had founded *The Dartmouth Review*. Fossedal's editorials in *The Washington Times,* which stressed the strategic defense arguments, were widely read in the Pentagon and the White House. General Graham's case had made it to the top, and President Reagan made his own case to the American people.

Thanks to Dan Graham, strategic defense already has some important allies, although it is not our national policy—yet. The President knows an extensive phalanx of entrenched opposition remains in the Congress, the press and, of course, in the Pentagon. Change, and especially fundamental change, does not come easily; and old strategies, even outdated and ill-advised ones, die hard.

Graham and Fossedal recognize that they have achieved an important objective: getting the President's attention, and with it the attention of the defense community. But their work has really just begun. Building such a defense and the consensus for it will require important changes, including a re-examination of the premises of our foreign policy, a re-ordering of the way weapons are ordered and produced (at least for the defensive systems themselves), and a major public effort to convince the Washington establishment that the technical and bureaucratic obstacles can be overcome.

A Defense That Defends outlines all of these basic steps that must be taken. It argues persuasively for the obvious moral and military merits of such a strategy, with a straightforward account of the hurdles that will have to be overcome. As one who is not an expert on weapons, I cannot say that every argument or every proposal herein propounded is sound. I *can* say that this book will inform you about one of the most important issues of our time. Our security and, indeed, our

survival are closely linked with the strategies our leaders decide upon, and this book makes a powerful case for a change
in the concepts and direction of those strategies. For this
reason alone, it deserves our serious attention.

Richard V. Allen, Distinguished Fellow,
The Heritage Foundation and Former
National Security Advisor to President Reagan.

A DEFENSE
THAT DEFENDS

I

The Coming
Strategic Debate

A SUDDEN FLARE-UP OF TENSIONS in the Middle East . . . A
breakdown in the tenuous stability of the Eastern bloc . . . An
overnight coup and political turnaround in a Third World
country . . .

America and the Soviet Union send in advisers to review
the unfolding events. The two sides begin to lift vital equipment and supplies to local allies. Suddenly, local guerrillas
launch an attack on a convoy of U.S. forces. The U.S. fires
back, hitting not only the guerrillas but also several Soviet
advisers. Direct shots are exchanged between American and
soviet troops . . . then, more shots.

From here, it is easy to extrapolate: The Soviets, fearing an
American strike on their military bases in the area, launch a
limited attack on American nuclear missiles. The Americans
fire off part of their reserve before an anticipated Kremlin
followup strike can occur. Moscow, Kiev, and Vladivostok
are gone. Then New York, Chicago, San Diego, Paris, London, Oslo, Rome—the spark set off by initially small events
ends in a fiery holocaust of nuclear destruction.

Every reasonable man and woman on the planet carries
about with him some vision of this nightmare. One does not
have to believe that the human race consists of paranoid
nuclear scenarists to know that the threat of nuclear war has
impressed itself deeply upon the human consciousness.

3

It is probably no overstatement to point out that the possibility of such a conflict is the central political, psychological, ethical reality of our time—that is, the one thing that most sets off this age from any other. Should Harry Truman have dropped the bomb on Japan? Did the United States face a growing "missile gap" as the calendar pushed on into the 1960s? Ought the Senate to have ratified the SALT I agreement, as it did, or the SALT II agreement, as it did not? Were Richard Nixon and Barry Goldwater trigger-happy? Jimmy Carter and George McGovern too timid? The nuclear defense debate has subliminally dominated the political agenda for three decades, with profound consequences.

Our very language reflects the recognition of the significance of the nuclear question. We live in "the nuclear age." We fear a confrontation of the two "superpowers." One can hardly read through a magazine or newspaper article without stumbling across the argot of the nuclear era: the "precipice," the "button," the "freeze," and the "ability to blow up the world several times over."

Like it or not, we seem pretty much stuck with a world in which diplomats and generals, congressmen and presidents, and, thus, to some degree, the public, must regularly think about the unthinkable.

This is a book about the unthinkable. But it offers a totally different ending to the scenario drawn above. It offers a different answer to the question, "What if the button is pushed?" It offers a totally different approach to how we avoid the "What if?" altogether. This, in short, is a look at the prospects of, and arguments for and against, an American defense against nuclear weapons: a defense that defends.

Many Americans, knowing that we have our own stockpile of nuclear weapons, believe that we *have* a defense. And we do, of sorts: a defense that threatens to blow up millions of Russian people if their government decides first to blow up millions of Americans. Stop and think, though. What happens to all our offensive missiles if the Soviets decide to attack anyway? What happens if many of them are blown up in their own silos? What happens if, though they remain intact, an American president faces 150 million casualties and has recourse only to inflict the same punishment on millions of innocent Russians?

For two years, a growing number of Americans have demanded an alternative—a different approach to the threat of nuclear war. Some formed the nuclear freeze movement, urging that the U.S. and the Soviet Union simply stop producing weapons. But they seem to have little idea how to impose this solution on the Soviets, or of how a world frozen at current levels of destructiveness would be any safer.

There is, however, another choice, different from both the quixotic call to disarmament and the hardliners' demands for more and more offense. The world that spawned the technology to destroy millions of people has spawned the technology to save them, even if such weapons are used. In space there is the opportunity to shoot down intercontinental missiles as they arc toward American cities. In the air, there is the opportunity to seize on American technological superiority to effectively screen out cities from a bomber attack. On the ground, there are new possibilities for inexpensive ABM measures and civil defense programs.

America has not even examined such options in any systematic way since the beginning of the anti-ballistic missile, or ABM, treaty banning such defense in 1972. Thus, even from the standpoint of historical and technological prudence, it is long overdue. Who knows what new systems, what new approaches, may have become possible in the eleven years since the 1972 pact was approved?

An examination of options and new approaches becomes all the more urgent in light of President Ronald Reagan's comments of March 23, 1983, in a speech that prompted a renaissance in the strategic debate—a debate that will dominate the strategic agenda for the next decade.

"If the Soviet Union will join with us in our effort to achieve major arms reduction," the President said, "we will have succeeded in stabilizing the nuclear balance. Nevertheless, it will still be necessary to rely on the specter of retaliation—on mutual threat, and that is a sad comment on the human condition.

"Would it not be better to save lives than to avenge them? Are we not capable of demonstrating our peaceful intentions by applying all our abilities and our ingenuity to achieving a truly lasting stability?

"After careful consultation with my advisers, including the

Joint Chiefs of Staff, I believe there is a way. Let me share with you a vision of the future which offers hope. It is that we embark on a program to counter the awesome Soviet military threat with measures that are defensive. Let us turn to the very strengths in technology that spawned our great industrial bases and that have given us the quality of life we enjoy today.

"Up until now we have increasingly based our strategy of deterrence upon the threat of retaliation. But what if free people could live secure in the knowledge that their security did not rest upon the threat of instant U.S. retaliation to deter a Soviet attack? [What if] we could intercept and destroy strategic ballistic missiles before they reached our own soil or that of our allies? . . ." (Full text appears in Appendix C.)

The response to the speech was breathtaking. White House reports indicated that the talk on defense, from which little of startling import was expected, received the largest and most positive flood of letters and calls of any speech that President Reagan has given. It touched off comment from virtually every major newspaper columnist in the country; television was packed with editorials, features, and technical reports; cover stories appeared in *Time* and *Newsweek* magazines; and Soviet chief of state Yuri Andropov issued a blistering statement. All this, one must remember, in reaction to a small part of the Reagan address—comments that read rather like an addendum or afterthought to the President's central theme concerning U.S.-Soviet forces, and the need for approval of his multi-year, multi-billion-dollar defense buildup.

Out of context, such a response could have been considered a tremendous overreaction. Think of it: America faces an armed foe with the potential to destroy most of its houses, cars, cities, and more than half its people. An American president, in turn, proposes that the country conduct *research* into the *idea* of *someday* building a defense against that threat. Dramatic changes in strategy ought to be made of more dramatic stuff.

In the context of established American nuclear thinking, however, even talk of a U.S. defense system was a significant event. The first thing to note, of course, is that to talk of replacing existing retaliatory strategies with a defense that defends is just that—talk.

Congress has not approved, nor the President asked for, any new programs of research into the technology of defense that are not already being funded. No talks have opened between the U.S. and the Soviets on revising or throwing out the ABM treaty, and the U.S. could not deploy a broad-based defense without either altering or violating its treaty commitments. Reagan was careful to remind his audience that the most publicized technology proposed for creating such a defense is ten, perhaps as long as 50 years off—though whether the country must actually wait that long for defense, or can build one now, using approaches that eschew laser beams and other Star Wars technology, is a subject of intense debate. What the President announced was not a new strategy, but the hope of a new strategy with potential new programs.

Much of the significance of proposing a defense against nuclear weapons, though, lies in the fact that those weapons, even if they are never fired, touch the very essence of our culture. The thought of escaping from the grip of such weapons is enough to liberate the human spirit. Instead of enduring a never-ending stalemate with nuclear arsenals always waiting to go off, we find a way to make those arsenals as obsolete as the crossbow. Instead of threatening to blow up the Soviet Union if the Soviet Union blows us up first, we simply threaten to protect ourselves. The near-consensus is that whatever we find in the search for an alternative to the current strategy of Mutual Assured Destruction—MAD—the search is most assuredly worth conducting. Analysts as typically diverse as Meg Greenfield and William F. Buckley, Jr., *National Review* and the *New Republic, The Washington Post* and *The Washington Times,* have agreed on that point. The coming debate over strategy becomes all the more significant, moreover, when you take into account all the assumptions, policies, and careers linked in some way to the present MAD approach.

There are clear technological issues: Can we knock down a missile or a bomber? Can the Russians knock down what we put up to knock them down? And what will it all cost? Many of the answers to these questions depend on the degree of our commitment to the defensive approach. There is little doubt in the scientific community that the U.S. can, at some point, develop the systems needed to do the job. But will we do it sooner, with the same sense of urgency that characterized the Apollo space program and, indeed, the Manhattan Project to build the atom bomb? Or do the technological risks argue for a more cautious, restrained—but therefore more costly—approach? President Reagan, probably wisely, held such questions in abeyance by offering no specific hardware or research programs in the aftermath of his speech. But they have already surfaced and, for some, constitute the heart of the debate.

Prudence dictates, moreover, that we address the question of how we arrived at the strategy of assured destruction in the first place. It is easy to ridicule the MAD strategy, with its Strangelovian implications, now that it has evolved. It is more important to go back and see how and why it evolved. MAD, like so many other strategic arrangements—our NATO alliance, our involvement in Central America, for example—is less the product of any one decision than of a series of decisions. If MAD is a bad strategy, then at what points were the bad premises laid for its construction? And how can we hope for a change from MAD, even if we desire it, if many of those premises remain intact?

There are the military issues. MAD deterrence analysis is the lens through which we typically view the nuclear balance of power equation; but if MAD is not the best way of looking at that equation, then what kind of U.S.-Soviet balance do we see when a sharper lens is used? What has MAD itself done to the balance of power: Has the strategy strengthened America by stirring fears of unpreparedness for war, weakened it by fanning fears of doomsday, or had no effect at all?

There are the foreign policy issues. What would the end of assured destruction mean for the future of arms control talks—and would we even need them in an age of defense? How would America's allies react to the new U.S. strategy? Assuming such a defense was based partly in space, as it probably would, what extra geopolitical advantage might accrue to the countries that move to exploit its possibilities for defense? What economic benefits? Would a defense based in space be a secure, peace-preserving blanket, or a dangerous first step toward a broader, Space Wars nightmare?

What will the Soviets do—try to knock down our defense? Build their own? Build still more offensive weapons?

Inasmuch as the debate covers such wide territory, it is necessary to think in broad terms when we evaluate the idea of a true defense against nuclear war. A true defense is not just a technical decision over this-or-that laser beam or a simpler satellite system. It is not just a question of what the ABM or any other treaty allows in precise legal jargon.

David Wilson of the *Boston Globe* captured the breadth of the coming debate when he wrote, in March 1982, that strategic defense might be the "economic, political, technical, and philosophical issue of the decade." Only when all these considerations are taken into account can one path, the path of defense, be compared to the other—the path of offense and arms control, wedded as they have been for 35 years under the overarching strategic reality of Mutual Assured Destruction.

Both hawkish Pentagon generals and ardent nuclear freeze supporters will no doubt cringe at the suggestion that their approaches go hand in hand. Their respective agendas could hardly be more diametrically opposite: build more on the one hand, build no more, and perhaps get rid of what we now have, on the other. That does not mean, however, that the two approaches are not based on the same assumptions, or that the two groups, the traditional hawks and the traditional doves, do not share a common resistance to defense.

Both approaches, for example, make some similar assumptions about the character of Soviet leadership; that it is at least rational, and thus will refrain from risking some of its population by launching a nuclear attack on the U.S. The offensive buildup position assumes this because it assumes that the MAD doctrine will keep the peace, so long as we maintain sufficient offensive power of our own to absorb a Soviet attack and to strike back with awesome destructiveness of our own. The arms limitation position assumes that the Soviet leadership can eventually be wheedled and cajoled into seeing its true self-interest (as perceived by the West) and thus agree to arms limitations and, eventually, arms reductions.

A defense strategy, by contrast, says that we had better trust ourselves, and make peaceful preparations to limit the harm any country can inflict on us.

We might also note that, politically, both the offense-only strategy school and the arms control school grew out of, and now feed into the continuation of MAD strategy. MAD, after all, imposes a tremendous burden on both parties. For in a world where our defense depends on our ability to retaliate, a diminuation in that retaliatory power threatens our very survival. We have seen just such a reduction in recent years, as the Soviet Union constructed a missile force capable of knocking ours out of its silos with warheads to spare, and, arguably, built other systems capable of blunting much of our remaining bomber and submarine forces. And in a world with the potential for such ineffable destruction, the drive to eliminate such weapons becomes not just a cause, but a moral imperative.

Defense, by contrast, undercuts both the need for future offensive buildups, at least to the degree now thought necessary, and the immediate danger to peace posed by the very existence of nuclear weapons.

This is not to ridicule either of the alternatives that have, until now, been offered to the American people. They are eminently rational, if we start from the assumption that defense is impossible. So, too, has the reaction of the American people, to the choices offered them, been sane and logical. Many observers in government, the media, and elsewhere—the policy elite—find great mystery in the shifts in public opinion on military matters, a particularly volatile process in the last few years.

In 1980, convinced that America's military capability had slipped dangerously, the people elected Ronald Reagan president on a broad platform calling for large increases in military spending. Two years later, with such a program barely underway, voters showed up all across the country to back the nuclear freeze resolution, saying, in effect, that enough was enough, America had, presumably, regained its position of strength, and it was now time to stop the arms race once and for all.

These and similar gyrations can be viewed as a series of left-right tilts: comparable to the desire to pull back after World War II, to alarm over the communist threat in Korea, to weariness with Korea, to involvement again in Vietnam, disgust with Vietnam, disgust with Iran and American weakness, and so on and so on. These swings are more likely, however, a simple reflection of the ambivalence imposed by the threat of nuclear destruction. Democracies are not known for their ability to calibrate finely; one of the oft-repeated lessons of Vietnam is that the American people cannot support a limited war. Yet MAD strategy demands just such a high-wire act from America's leaders and its people. On the one hand, we must face a threatening foe with a steel-like determination to maintain the nuclear balance. On the other, we must, for ourselves and the world, seek to negotiate with that foe lest the demented drive to superiority, or parity, end in countless deaths.

What the American people seem to be asking for is an alternative. And defense, in many ways, seems to provide one. If strategic defense has remained off the agenda by its implicit threat to both the disarmers and the rearmers, so defense, now on the agenda, offers a hope of a strategic consensus.

Defense offers the peace marcher one of his most cherished hopes: a world free of the threat of total nuclear annihilation. It offers the Pentagon general the fond dream of an America no longer subject to the blackmail of MAD. There are serious objections to a program of defense, objections that will be dealt with. But the intuitive reaction of most Americans is bound to be: Let's try it.

II

How We Went MAD

Whentext text text WHEN WE SPEAK OF A "DEFENSE" against nuclear weapons, it is clear enough what is meant: a system of guns and satellites and civil defense plans to blunt the impact of a nuclear strike. One of the great burdens of MAD strategy, however, is that it blurs such terminology, treating our offensive missiles as defensive, on the one hand, and suggesting that defenses, on the other hand, might be offensive—by making one side, or both, more likely to launch an offensive attack, secure in the knowledge that its cities and people are essentially protected.

There is nothing illegitimate about this line of reasoning so long as we remain within the paradigm of assured destruction. If the threat to destroy Soviet citizens and industrial capacity is our sole protection against their weapons, then that is our "defense." That destructive, offensive capacity is what protects our country, because it convinces the Russians never to launch their own arsenal. Meanwhile, active and passive defensive measures on our part are, at best, of only marginal utility, because it is our ability to inflict punishment after a strike, rather than our capacity to blunt a strike, that is going to deter a Soviet attack.

But suppose—just suppose—that the system of deterrence breaks down. Suppose a nuclear war starts. Then the distinction between "defensive" and "offensive" systems becomes clear. Once a war starts, our offensive weapons are of little use in protecting America's cities: The threat to unleash them has already failed; the Soviet missiles and bombers are on their way. Once a nuclear war starts, a defense would, in fact, be our critical strategic asset. If we had a strong air defense system, we might stop Russian bombers from reaching their targets. If we had an advantage in submarine detection, we could sink some Soviet subs before they could fire their missiles. If we had an anti-ballistic missile defense system, we could shoot down those Soviet missiles in mid-air. If we had a civil defense program, we could move our people away from the cities and from any stray warheads that might get through the defensive net.

For the purposes of our discussion, then, the terms "offensive" and "defensive" are used throughout the book in the sense they are used above. Because MAD strategy refuses or at least downplays such a distinction, the very use of such terminology invites controversy. But for the debate that is about to occur, reviving those distinctions is vital.

Both authors toured the country extensively in 1982 and 1983, talking and writing about the subject of a defense against nuclear weapons. Invariably, one of the first questions people asked was, "Why aren't we building a defense already? I thought we had a department of defense that was taking care of those things." And in the MAD sense, of course, we do. Why we do not have a defense in the defenseman's sense of the word, however, is the deeper and more important question.

One answer put forward is that the country achieved a strategic consensus in the late 1960s and early '70s that defense was a dangerous, destabilizing route to go. It would be hard to argue that such was not the consensus among American policy elites. The decision to eschew land-based and space-based ABMs was begun in the Eisenhower administration, continued through the Kennedy-Johnson years, institutionalized under Richard Nixon and the ABM treaty, and extended by Jimmy Carter's and Ronald Reagan's reaffirmation of the treaty under regular five-year reviews in 1977 and 1982. Clark Clifford, Lyndon Johnson's Secretary of Defense, spoke conventional wisdom when he wrote in his 1968 report to the Congress, "We remain convinced that we should continue to give primary priority in the allocation of available resources to the primary objective of our strategic forces, namely 'assured destruction.'"

Ten years after the defense debate presumably had been settled in the corridors of power—in such journals as *Foreign Affairs*, on editorial pages of leading newspapers, and in the halls of Congress and the White House—the American people continue to lean in the opposite direction. During the summer of 1982, Sidlinger and Associates, a respected polling firm, sampled public opinion on the question of a shift from assured destruction strategies and systems. Two out of three polled indicated that they didn't even know that the U.S. had abandoned efforts to defend itself against incoming missiles. Asked if this knowledge disturbed them, 57 percent answered "Yes, a great deal"; 23 percent answered, "Yes, somewhat"; and only 19 percent said "No, not very much," or "No, not at all." A full 86 percent said they thought the U.S. should change this approach and deploy an ABM defense; 10 percent disagreed. Perhaps most interesting, three of every four respondents said the cost of such a defense against nuclear attack would *not* be a "primary factor" in their decision to support or oppose such a system.

It is probably poetically just that a strategy that holds millions of Americans, Soviets, and people all over the world at nuclear gunpoint was debated and settled with little input from the hostages themselves. As the nuclear freeze and anti-freeze movements demonstrate, the subject of nuclear strategy evokes deep passions; it is not obvious that mass participation in the strategic debate would have ended in a more favorable result. The point is not whether a group of American politicians, think-tankers, and journalists conspired to keep American nuclear strategy out of the hands of the American people. Of course they didn't. To understand the evolution of MAD strategy, though, and its continued rejection of defensive solutions, we must first understand the character of the debate.

The relatively clear consensus of the American people is that defense must be pursued; the Sidlinger poll, which reveals that two-thirds of them believe it is being pursued, reflects their not unreasonable inclination to leave the particulars up to their leaders. This being the case, those particulars become crucially important. If technical officers in the Pentagon, for example, believe that defense is a low priority—the implicit message of MAD strategy—they will spend less time, energy, and lobbying expense researching and encouraging new programs to achieve it. If strategic thinkers see that arms talks are given the highest strategic priority—as they must be in a world of assured holocaust—they will be especially cautious about promoting an alternative. Again, they will not have to actively reject the idea of defense in order to play a major role in steering the country away from it. What sane arms negotiator or presidential adviser would risk upsetting delicate SALT or START talks with suggestions for a radically different American strategy?

The fact is, America went MAD not because of a conscious, explicit decision to reject defense; rather, the strategic debate unfolded as a series of *ad hoc* decisions: decisions about whether we could build a defense, what a defense would mean for arms control, how the allies might react, and so on. These decisions, in turn, were the outgrowth of assumptions and premises that could only lead away from defense and toward assured destruction. Politicians gave technicians no mandate to vigorously pursue defense, so, naturally, they pursued it with little vigor. Strategists, in turn, accepted the popular notion that a handful of bombs can destroy the world; hence they insisted that any defense less than perfect was no defense at all. Assured destruction strategy is rooted in these and other strategic canards, in ideas about the purpose and nature of defense that historically have been rejected by military thinkers but which have gained credence in the era of new destructive potential.

The seeds of assured destruction were planted in the years following Hiroshima, the heady postwar zenith of American power. Americans had some pangs of guilt, perhaps, about developing and using the bomb. Nevertheless, with traditional American optimism, they looked on the bright side. As the United States disengaged conventional forces from Europe and the Pacific after the war, nuclear weaponry seemed to offer a comfortable guarantee of American security. Hadn't the bomb just convinced the Japanese to sur-

render without a bloody fight to the finish? Had it not kept
the Soviets out of Western Europe despite a large Soviet
advantage in local forces? A handful of our bombers could
wipe any enemy "off the face of the earth." Even if other
countries should obtain this power, moreover, its
awesomeness seemed a further guarantee against war to begin with. No country would consider war as a serious alternative in this new age; perversely, invention of the bomb
seemed like a great advance for the cause of peace.

It was against this backdrop that the first, and the most
influential, treatise on nuclear war appeared in 1946: editor
Bernard Brodie's collection of essays, *The Absolute Weapon*.
The book foreshadowed much of the strategic thought that
has followed since; indeed, one can infer some of its conclusions from the very title. Brodie and his writers construct,
somewhat more elaborately than will be related here, the
familiar chain of logic surrounding the MAD debate. One
plane-load of nuclear bombs (the intercontinental missile did
not yet exist) can reduce New York City into "complete chaos
and horror." Therefore, any plans to defend New York, or
other American population centers, from hostile attack must
include the ability to wipe out any bomber that might reach
the city "before we can even speak of a defense against
atomic bombs being effective." (In other words, perfect defense or none.) Furthermore, such a defense is virtually impossible. Even the vaunted British air defense against the
Germans suffered heavy leakage. No matter how complete
the defense mechanism, some planes are certain to get
through. Brodie et al. even concluded that no perfect defense "can be envisioned."

Therefore, civilization had achieved the "ultimate
weapon." Talk of the balance of power, of strategy, of defense and offense were meaningless. Brodie says: "Superiority in airforces fails to guarantee security. . . . Superiority in
the number of bombs is no guarantee [of security], because if
2,000 bombs in the hands of either party is enough to destroy entirely the economy of the other, the fact that one side
has 6,000 and the other 2,000 will be of relatively low
significance."

Such observations were not only interesting but, in a way, comforting. Brodie's was not, of course, the first theory advanced arguing that new factors in technology or society had made war a thing of the past. Norman Angell's 1910 book, *The Great Illusion,* was the talk of Europe, with its thesis that "future war is impossible" because the economic linkages between European nations were so extensive that no state could hope to gain from war, much less sustain the effort if it tried. In a series of popular lectures at Cambridge, the esteemed Lord Escher echoed the argument. "The consequences of commercial disaster, financial ruin, and individual suffering would be so great," Escher told his spellbound audiences, "as to make conflict unthinkable." When World War I was finally fought, it was called "the war to end wars," ushering in a chain of mistakes that would make that phrase a self-undermining prophecy.

So, too, before World War II, the notion of assured destruction was widely accepted. German violations of the Versailles Treaty, which limited its land and air forces, and the London agreement, limiting its navy, were dismissed as strategically irrelevant. The British Defense Ministry concluded, for example, that Germany lacked the rubber and iron to sustain a war effort for more than three weeks. The calculaters did not know about Germany's growing synthetic rubber industries, and did not notice its strategic stockpiling programs. They did not consider that an early German war strategy might concentrate on vital factories in Czechoslovakia or sources of rare metals in Africa.

If doomsday talk after World War II contained an historical echo, though, it also held the same attraction it held for Europeans in the early 1900s and late 1930s. Offensive nuclear weapons offered a war-weary people "the ultimate weapon," a financially and psychologically cheap route to peace and security. Mass culture underlined the message that nuclear weapons were a freakshow. Movies played up the science fiction angle with tale of monsters and shrinking men and doomsday end-alls. Popular songs and books satirized The Bomb. (It is interesting to note, though, that the public's instinct was to take the nuclear threat seriously.

Government pamphlets advising where to go during a nuclear attack, how to build an underground attack shelter, and how to find out if food, water, and other necessities were contaminated were tremendously popular in the 1940s and '50s. Only decades of counterculture convinced Americans, unlike their counterparts in Switzerland, Denmark, and Japan, that nuclear war is so serious it can only be laughed at.)

Early proponents of proto-MAD strategy were given a severe jolt by events in Berlin and Korea, which seemed to refute their idea that the new realities of nuclear weaponry prevented conflict. The theory, however, was not discarded but revised. Henry Kissinger and other foreign policy analysts began writing "limited war" scenarios in which conflict still occurred, but was kept below the nuclear threshold by the tacit understanding of each side that to go too far threatened all-out confrontation. And since both Berlin and Korea were settled at the conventional level, without recourse to nuclear weapons, defenders correctly pointed out that neither situation offered a direct test of their thesis. These events forced qualification, but not rejection, of their ideas. As Kissinger later observed in his first book of memoirs, ". . . inherent in deterrence [is the fact] that one can never prove what has prevented aggression. Is it our defense posture? Or is it that our adversary never intended to attack in the first place?" The limited war explanation for conventional conflict can never be "disproven," because the proof against it, a nuclear war, will make the verdict decidedly anticlimactic. Nevertheless, a perceived erosion of American invulnerability ushered the Truman administration out of office, and ushered in the presidency of Dwight Eisenhower.

It was the Eisenhower administration that first gave the evolving American strategy of MAD a slogan: the New Look. The New Look's basic premise was that the Truman administration had failed not in overemphasizing, but underemphasizing nuclear weapons. America had failed, for example, to prevent the Soviet Union from developing its own nuclear program. It had neglected to use its influence in China. And it had concentrated its military dollars, oddly, on the relatively more expensive items of manpower and conventional weapons—on maintaining a costly residual force in Europe, for example, when the cheaper alternative of greater air power and nuclear forces offered a "bigger bang for the buck."

The New Look was thus a marriage of two important interests, a marriage that would be consummated under Robert McNamara in the 1960s. Interest one: It was cheap. American forces in Europe had already declined from 12.3 million in 1945 to 670, 000 in 1947, but the New Look promised the possibility of still further reductions in this expensive force with no concomitant reduction in Western security. Our tactical nuclear weapons, strategic bombers, and threats of massive retaliation would both deter war and throw back aggression if it was attempted.

Interest two: It was easy. The New Look downplayed the possibility of American deaths in future conflicts, suggesting a mechanization of the battlefield that would allow the U.S. to prevail without massive infusions of manpower. As one observer put it: "The theory of nuclear deterrence was particularly attractive to the new administration, which felt that it owed its election largely to the unpopularity of the protracted ground combat, long casualty lists, and high defense expenditures of the Korean War. It was claimed that the threat of nuclear retaliation, requiring mainly air power and nuclear weapons, in which the United States, at that time, enjoyed a tremendous advantage, would offset the manpower advantage of the communist world, thus reducing defense costs and limiting the number of young men who must sacrifice several years of their lives to military service." (James E. King, Jr., *National Security in the Nuclear Age*, New York: Frederick A. Praeger, 1960.)

The beginnings of MAD strategy, then, took root during a time of unquestioned American superiority. There were many questions about the useability of this superiority. It had not kept the communists out of Korea or Eastern Europe. It would not necessarily deter the communists' conventional forces from an assault on Western Europe, American threats of retaliation notwithstanding. There was no question, however, that America enjoyed a virtual monopoly of force at the nuclear level. Most of the Soviet Union's crude bombers were incapable of reaching the continental U.S. without several refueling stops. Heavy reliance on this branch of the military, in which the U.S. enjoyed such a significant advantage, was not only bound to be popular; it also made sense.

Even as American strategies of retaliation were forming, however, that foundation of superiority on which they were based was eroding. Much of the public's acquiescence in strategies of massive retaliation, remember, was based on the fact that they were one-sided: We had a situation of unilateral, not mutual, assured destruction. That situation was changing. As early as 1951, it became clear that the Soviet Union planned to emulate America's buildup. American capacity would hit a pre-Kennedy plateau in 1955 with the completion of some 200 B-37 bombers and more than 1,000 B-47s, supplementing an initial force of only a few hundred bombs.

Soviet efforts were just beginning as Ike took office, and outgoing Secretary of State Dean Acheson warned: "We have a substantial lead in air power and in atomic weapons. . . . But with the pressure of time, even though we continue our advantage in the field the value of their lead diminishes."

Soon after his inauguration, Eisenhower spoke of a potential "atomic armaments race" that would eliminate America's monopoly. "The expenditure of vast sums for weapons of defense can guarantee absolute safety for the cities and citizens of no nation," he said. "The awful arithmetic of the atomic bomb does not permit any such easy solution. Even against the most powerful defense, an aggressor in possession of the effective minimum number of atomic bombs for a surprise attack would probably place a sufficient quantity of his bombs on the chosen targets to cause hideous damage."

As late as 1962, the nuclear balance would be tested, at least indirectly. Though the Cuban missile crisis has been the object of several recent controversies and historical revisions, the general consensus is that American nuclear superiority, as Robert Kennedy wrote in *Thirteen Days: A Memoir of the Cuban Missile Crisis* (New York: W. W. Norton & Co., 1971), determined the chain of events in America's favor. Yet as early as the late 1950s, Soviet advancements were sufficient to cause fears of a growing missile gap, with the U.S. on the short end. The 1960 Kennedy-Nixon race focused attention on the defense issue in an important and unusual way.

America under Eisenhower continued to spend an impressive 10 percent of its Gross National Product, and virtually half of the federal budget, on the military, compared to five to six percent of GNP, and less than a third of the budget, in the 1970s. Eisenhower initiated important improvements in American forces, the development of the Polaris submarine and Minuteman missile, two systems that remain the foundation of the U.S. strategic triad.

When John F. Kennedy took office in 1961, America still possessed effective first-strike capability. Yet Kennedy's campaign assaulted Richard Nixon for his role in a "dangerous inattention" to national security. Significantly, the heart of Kennedy's attacks was not the need for a "pay any price, bear any burden" approach to the military budget, though this was included. Rather, JFK questioned the whole strategic framework of the Eisenhower years. He attacked the doctrine of massive retaliation as inflexible, making U.S. power "irrelevant," and urged what would become the strategic approach of "flexible response."

In the closest thing to a direct vote on strategies of retaliation the U.S. has seen, Americans chose an alternate course. A strategy of flexible response would require, as Kennedy Defense Secretary Robert McNamara later explained, "unchallenged superiority at every level of force." It was not enough for America to be stronger than its potential adversaries on balance, or in certain areas. The needs of security in a nuclear age required that the U.S. be able to prevail in any kind of conflict. If the Soviets launched a naval battle in the Middle East, we should be able to defeat them on the seas. If they launched a ground assault in Europe, the U.S. and its allies should be able to win on the ground. McNamara explained the change:

> The defense establishment we found in 1961 was based on a strategy of massive nuclear retaliation as the answer to all military and political aggression. We, however, were convinced that our enemies would never find credible a strategy which even the American people did not believe.

We believed in a strategy of controlled, flexible response, where the military forces of the United States would become a finely tuned instrument of national policy, versatile enough to meet with appropriate force the full spectrum of possible threats to our national security from guerrilla subversion to all-out nuclear war.

What the Kennedy administration envisioned, in other words, was a true strategy: a coherent plan for the constructive use of American force throughout the globe; a conceptual framework for the application of power. In the buoyant mood of New Frontierism, the Kennedy White House saw America as a positive force in the world, and sought to increase American influence by developing a strategy to fit our opportunities for influence.

President Kennedy's plans for a military to meet the new strategy were equally bold. Half-again the number of Polaris submarines. Double the production capacity of the Minuteman missile. Place more than one-third of the country's 1,700 bombers on 15-minute alert. Beef up American conventional forces with several new conventional equipment advances.

Most significant for our purposes was the stress that such an approach allowed to be placed upon defense. After all, Kennedy's was initially a strategy for the use of power. A nuclear defense strengthened America's domestic resolve to stick with the program, and increased the credibility of our pledge to contain Soviet aggression at whatever level necessary. Flexible response made the use of power thinkable, and thinkable power calls for a defense.

Hence, during McNamara's first year as Secretary of Defense, he ordered development of a missile system (NIKE-X) to protect the U.S. population against enemy aircraft and missiles. He advocated a significant program of civil defense. He changed targeting procedures: Should a nuclear war break out, the U.S. did not plan as a first option to wipe out Soviet cities. Rather, the McNamara strategy envisioned a counterforce attack on Soviet weaponry, designed to minimize the damage that Russian offensive forces could do to the United States.

"The United States has come to the conclusion that to the extent [that it is] feasible, basic military strategy in a possible general war should be approached in much the same way that more conventional military operations have been regarded in the past," McNamara said in a landmark speech at Ann Arbor, Michigan. "That is to say, principal military objectives, in the event of nuclear war . . . should be the destruction of the enemy's military forces, not of his civilian population."

The new strategy sought to avoid war by seriously planning for it. The doctrine understood that even overwhelming U.S. capacity might not guarantee that nuclear war could never occur—the result, perhaps, of miscalculation by an enemy, escalation from a conventional stalemate by a frustrated government, or even a simple nuclear accident, an inadvertent launch by some hostile power.

Even a missile gap that favored America "does not guarantee that a nuclear war cannot take place," said McNamara. "Not only do nations sometimes act in ways that are hard to explain on a rational basis, but even when acting in a 'rational' way they sometimes, indeed, disturbingly often, act on the basis of misunderstandings of the true facts of a situation. They misjudge the way the others will react and the way others will interrupt what they are doing."

The doctrine, simply, allowed for an American defense. It answered the question, "What do we do if deterrence breaks down?" First, we limit the damage Soviet forces can do by attacking Soviet forces as a top priority—rather than Soviet cities first, weapons later. Next, we combine an active anti-bomber and anti-missile defense with a passive civil defense program. Finally, we give the Soviets every reason to limit a nuclear conflict to a military-to-military exchange—that is, a battle to destroy the other's forces—by consciously avoiding an all-out attack on Soviet population centers. True, once the nuclear threshold was crossed, all-out war might be unavoidable. But it might not. America's evolving strategy of counterforce and flexible response seized every possible opportunity to avoid the holocaust of an eye-for-an-eye exchange of civilian massacre. The United States was well on the way to a balanced strategy for deterring nuclear war—by taking the prudent step of preparing for every possible means of Soviet attack.

Yet, as Secretary McNamara and the Johnson administration left office, the rosy plans of the Kennedy campaign had been abandoned. Flexible pressure had failed to contain communism in Vietnam, and had, in fact, fomented growing domestic opposition to American defense policies. Plans for an American buildup had come to a near freeze in the final five years of McNamara's reign, and all the while the Russians were building. Defensive American systems were scrapped as it became clear that the Soviets were nearing parity: Such systems, it was feared, would only upset the emerging balance between U.S. and Soviet forces. Threatened with such a return to American superiority, the Soviets would either be tempted into a quick strike or would match American defense with Soviet offense in a never-ending spiral of nuclear arms production.

We had, in short, adopted a strategy of Mutual Assured Destruction. And while the new framework of MAD did not constrain the Soviets—they continued to press ahead with plans to protect their own population from American weapons—it put a virtual cap on the defensive measures the American government was willing to pursue.

America's drift from the initial strategy of flexible response to the full enshrinement of MAD represents the seminal event in strategic thinking, because it was Kennedy's administration that offered the greatest hope of leading America away from the dead-end alternative of MAD. Even though the U.S. and its people desired a change in strategy, and, in fact, *began* such a change, America wound up more reliant than ever before on offensive retaliation as a defense. The failure to follow the course that Kennedy set out carries lessons for the strategic defense debate today, for it is a debate that will be fought along many of the same battle lines.

What happened between 1960 and 1968, when Clark Clifford announced a return to our "mutual destruction element," and Lyndon Johnson urged the Soviets to agree to a joint ban on all defensive strategic systems?

For one thing, Vietnam happened. America's nightmare in Southeast Asia spoke to the limits of power as against the New Frontier optimism of the early Kennedy administration. It corresponded to a time of domestic turmoil and doubt. America began to question its own legitimacy. The broad reaction against real and perceived injustices by America manifested itself partly in distaste for American power in general. No country that experiences the internal divisions that America experienced as the decade of the '60s dragged on is likely to view the rest of the world with the confidence needed to match an aggressive, self-confident opponent like the Soviet Union.

Accompanying these doubts were doubts about the world order America helped shape after World War II. How such doubts evolved, given the successes of the Marshall Plan, the rebuilding of Japan, the limited victory of the United Nations containment action in Korea, and a whole host of stunning development successes in the Third World, spurred on by American technology, is enigmatic. There is no question, however, that the doubts were there. It was as if, once we realized that the world was not black and white, with America infallibly in the right and Russia unalterably in the wrong, we completely lost our ability to distinguish between the different shades of grey. MAD suggests that no one dare even think about nuclear war; it thus corresponded to a deeper notion that took root in the Vietnam era, namely, that no one dare even think about power. He who uses it may do some good, but he may also err; he who declines to act need not accept responsibility.

A second, more concrete pressure behind the transition from flexible response to MAD was a very real change in the balance of power. The two, in a sense, went hand in hand. MAD strategy suggested that, beyond a certain level, fresh increments of strategic power were meaningless; growing Soviet power, on the other hand, suggested that our only hope for avoiding holocaust lay in the grey, lurid area of mutual deterrence. The one reinforced the other in a grim synergism. But the Soviets would have gained in power even if the most ambitious Kennedy buildup plans had been implemented.

Thus, by the end of the decade, America faced a situation in which a rough balance of power seemed inevitable. Given the significant stockpiles that existed on each side, MAD offered a simpler, cheaper way of defense by deterrence than defense by defense. Respected historians and foreign policy advisers suggested that balance was all the Russians wanted; if that was so, our wisest course was simply to maintain the rough balance in offensive firepower until the logic of arms control became evident to the Kremlin, and the futility of further arms buildups clear. With the growth of Soviet power, America faced two options: start building expensive, imperfect, ground-based defenses, or hope for arms control and accept a vision of limited American influence under the unsatisfactory, but seemingly unavoidable framework of MAD.

At the time—prior to a decade of further Soviet expansion, greater Soviet repression, and repeated Soviet treaty violations—the country's choice to eschew a defense was understandable. It does not seem so now. There were technological and cost limits that do not exist today. Ground-based anti-missile stations, in order to protect the country, must blanket a nation of millions of square miles. The options emerging for the 1980s call for point systems on the ground, but only as a limited backup to a cheap, easily deployed defense in space. At far lower cost, and with greater protection, American satellites can cover Soviet missile ranges, as we will describe later. The McNamara people did not have, or at least did not consider, this option.

They did have, however, the opportunity to move *toward* the more complete defense envisioned today. As McNamara's comment on one proposed ABM defense reveals, the administration's decision to go with MAD and reject defense had as much to do with bad strategy as with a shortage of cash:

> It is important to understand that none of the ABM systems at the present or more forseeable state of the art would provide an impenetrable shield over the United States. Were such a shield possible, we would certainly want it—and we would certainly build it. . . . If we could build and deploy a genuinely impenetrable shield over the United States, we would be willing to spend not $40 billion but any reasonable multiple of that amount that was necessary. The money in itself is not the problem; the penetrability of the proposed shield is the problem.

If money, *per se*, was not a problem, the budget, in the true sense of the word, was. A budget is a series of expenditures designed to meet a certain set of needs. How we view those needs, how we structure priorities, is crucial in determining what items we consider worth buying and what items we decide against. And McNamara's view of American strategic needs assigned low priority to defense, in the operative sense. Unless we could build a perfect, "impenetrable" defense, we had no use for a defense at all. Protecting 60 million Americans is no better than protecting none; we must protect all or have nothing. MAD strategy dictated spending decisions by throwing into question the whole utility of strategic defense.

Defenses throughout military history have been designed to make attack more difficult and more costly—not impossible. There is no "absolute shield" against the bullet. But a bulletproof vest can reduce the risk of the damage done by an attack. Defenses, by making the outcome of conflict uncertain for the aggressor, have often prevented attack just as surely as "assured destruction." General Grant put a cavalry screen in front of his forces not because the cavalry was invulnerable to Confederate fire, or because a few hundred horsemen could defeat 20,000 of General Lee's soldiers, but because he did not want the battle to commence with an assault on his main forces. The Belgians, in World War I, endured tremendous suffering in order to merely slow down the German advance by a matter of days. Those days, however, proved critical, allowing the battered French army time to regroup for the defense of Paris.

Under MAD notions of nuclear conflict, then, unrealistic expectations must be met before a defense becomes even rational. Under McNamara, the Pentagon also adopted the idea of "cost-benefit analysis" for evaluating military projects and deciding which ones to initiate, continue, or discontinue. On one level, it is hard to understand how this concept could be applied to the military at all. What is the "benefit" of a defense system that saves millions of American lives? How does it guide us in evaluating the costs? Of course, it is of little help at all. What cost-benefit analysis can do is aid us in deciding between different systems designed to accomplish the same goal. At its base, it simply means "if two systems do the same job equally well, use the cheaper one."

In combination with MAD, however, cost-benefit analysis helped nudge America away from systems of a defensive nature. It is cheaper to build another offensive missile than it is to defend a city. If "defense" can be based on a nuclear arsenal sufficient to destroy the Soviet Union, defending people carries almost no "benefit" at all. McNamara thus changed the Pentagon's focus from strategy to accounting. It became commonplace to talk in terms of "buying" a certain level of deterrence. The key component of the acronym MAD (Mutual Assured Destruction) is the last word: destruction. Anything that fails to add to our destructive capacity, our deterrent, is an "inefficient input" in the military budget.

Indeed, the defense establishment came to embrace MAD not just because of the historical factors, not just because of the growing Soviet threat, and not just because it was an efficient way of protecting, at least ostensibly, the country. MAD was embraced, and a nuclear defense rejected, because to the chosen few who were debating these questions, the idea of a nuclear defense was dangerous.

Critics charged that weapons for damage-limiting counterforce could, in turn, be aimed at the Soviet Union in a disarming first strike. They were right, though they failed to explain how Soviet development of that same counterforce capability which we deliberately avoided failed to constitute an equal threat.

The analysts said that a doctrine that emphasized reducing the damage of nuclear war reduced its horrors. Nuclear war thus becomes thinkable—something you can plan for, hoping to avoid, but ready to meet if necessary. The analysts failed to notice that wars throughout history have been initiated more by the failure to take war seriously than by an unwillingness to contemplate it. Planning to defend ourselves reduces the Soviet advantage in striking; at the same time, it alerts us to war's horrors by forcing us to deal with them rationally.

Whatever other forces were at work throughout the Kennedy-Johnson-McNamara years, the result finally was the acceptance of the very doctrine of massive response and assured destruction that once seemed avoidable. In 1968, McNamara summed up his nuclear doctrine:

I am convinced that our forces must be sufficiently large to possess an "Assured Destruction" capability. By this I mean an ability to inflict at all times and under all foreseeable conditions an unacceptable degree of damage upon any single aggressor, or a combination of aggressors—even after absorbing a surprise attack. One can add many refinements to this basic concept, but the fundamental principle involved is simply this: It is the clear and present ability to destroy the attacker as a viable 20th century notion and unwavering will to use these forces in retaliation to a nuclear attack upon ourselves that provides the deterrent, and not the ability partially to limit damage to ourselves.

With MAD as our accepted nuclear strategy, it is easy to understand the repeated decisions in the 1970s to forego nuclear defense. The doctrine of leaving our cities vulnerable to Russian missiles was settled. Hence, the ABM system was delayed under the Johnson administration, limited by the ABM treaty under Nixon, and scrapped under Ford. Research for the ABM declined under Presidents Ford and Carter.

This is not to say that the ABM treaty, signed in 1972, (see Appendix B) was inevitable. The blame or credit for that pact ought to lie primarily with the American leaders who supported it: Richard Nixon, Henry Kissinger, and the U.S. Senate. The enshrinement of MAD, at least as American policy, was, however, a predictable result of changes in the balance of power, in American resolve, and technology. For a brief time in the 1970s, each side possessed roughly the same number of offensive missile launchers. Weapons knowhow had advanced to the point where each side had a large arsenal of weapons accurate enough to score a sure hit against a city, but too inaccurate to make hitting the other side's missile silos likely. America had virtually no strategic defense system; the Soviets had a massive civil and air defense program, but as yet lacked the sophisticated technology to deploy a broad-based population defense against strategic missiles.

By 1972 and the signing of the ABM treaty, though, that window of opportunity was rapidly closing. The "MIRVing" of missiles with several warheads made it theoretically possible for each side to simultaneously possess a first-strike capability. (Suppose each side has, say, 100 missiles tipped with 500 warheads. Only three warheads typically must be targeted on an opposing missile to score a certain hit. So either side can eliminate the other's entire force by launching 300 warheads, or 60 missiles. That leaves the attacker with almost half his force and a nuclear monopoly.) Soviet advances in submarine detection and bomber intercept tactics threw into question the other two legs of America's retaliatory triad.

Perhaps the greatest argument against MAD strategy is what happened to the balance of power during the height of the MAD era: The ten years following the signing of the ABM treaty in 1972 was a decade marked by a weakening in American defense and resolve in general, and, in particular, by a growing "window of [nuclear] vulnerability," as Defense Secretary Harold Brown put it in 1979. Was MAD strategy, in fact, a cause of America's military decline? That is a question well worth addressing, and plausibly answered, "Yes."

III

MAD and the
Balance of Power

SOUTH YEMEN. IRAQ. MOZAMBIQUE. Somalia. Ethopia.
Angola. India. Laos. Cambodia. Vietnam. Iran. Libya.
Nicaragua.

The world became a dangerous place with the decline of
American influence in the Nixon-Carter era. We saw brutal
regimes take root against a backdrop of violence and terror
in the Middle East. The United States ceded its rights to
control the Panama Canal, then watched as Cuban and
Soviet arms fomented revolt in Nicaragua, El Salvador, and
Honduras. To a Soviet invasion of the small and peaceful
country of Afghanistan, we responded with an Olympic boy-
cott. To massive Soviet violations of the chemical weapons
ban (see Appendix A), the Helsinki human rights accords,
and the SALT I and II treaties, we responded with verbal
diplomatic protest—in the case of SALT, not even that: To
identify and prosecute Soviet violations of these arms agreements, it was thought, might undermine the prospects for
meaningful arms negotiations.

These and other events did not take place in a military
vacuum. The Soviets use the term "correlation of forces" to
describe the ebb and flow of power in the world. The term
"correlation" indicates their understanding of how broad an
idea power really is. It includes political will and legitimacy:
The prince who is loved by his people, Machiavelli wrote, can

31

control even princes of greater wealth and stature who can-not.

Economic power, too, is a force. The power to produce widgets is the power to produce widget-guns. At the base, though, the correlation of forces consists of military might—because, if correctly and judiciously applied, this might can be used to acquire vital resources, sap the morale of an oppo-nent, and intimidate weak and neutral nations.

As the Vietnam years drew to a close, it became clear that the Soviets had become the premier military power in the world. As early as 1969, Melvin Laird, then Secretary of Defense, testified that the Soviets surpassed the U.S. in strategic missile launchers. It was one year later that Soviet dictator Leonid Brezhnev declared that a "rough equality of forces exists." Since that time, the U.S. has unilaterally dis-mantled almost 30 percent of its total nuclear force in order to comply with various SALT I and SALT II requirements. We have deployed no new missile; the Soviets, four. Our counterforce capability has remained relatively constant; the Soviet Union's increased by a factor of three-to-five. ("Coun-terforce" capability simply measures the raw nuclear power one side can use against the other in terms of destruc-tiveness, instead of relying on the less important mea-surements of numbers of missiles and delivery vehicles, or numbers of warheads, typically used.)

By 1979, Secretary of Defense Harold Brown was warning of the window of vulnerability of all American missiles. For-mer Secretary of State Henry Kissinger told the Senate Foreign Relations Committee that year, "Rarely in history has a nation so passively accepted such a radical change in the military balance. If we are ready to remedy it, we must first recognize the fact that we have placed ourselves at a significant disadvantage voluntarily."

As members of both political parties and all political per-suasions began to look at the emerging figures, the nuclear threat came into stark view. America faced a looming 7–1 Soviet counterforce capability; projections indicated that by 1985 the Soviets would be able to launch seven warheads at every American missile. Those heavy Soviet missiles would give the Kremlin an overall 5–1 edge in total throw weight, and, despite American efforts to catch up with the Soviets, a 3–1 or 4–1 advantage in total re-entry vehicles. (Figures from David S. Sullivan, *The Bitter Fruits of Salt,* Austin, Texas: University of Texas Press, 1982.) As former President Nixon predicted in *The Real War* (New York: Warner Books, 1980):

> The damage to our strategic stability and to our security will be a self-inflicted wound. By 1982 . . . our [missile] force will be thoroughly vulnerable to a first strike; our aging [bomber] force, of which only 20 percent is kept loaded and on ground alert, will be vulnerable on the ground and en route to target; our stratetic warning and communication system will be susceptible to attack and disruption (through Soviet anti-satellite measures); and Soviet anti-submarine warfare capabilities may not permit smug confidence in the survivability over time of our submarines at sea, approximately 50 percent of the force. In any case, the specter of an overwhelming Soviet strategic reserve—at least ten times our own after a first strike—would reduce the threat of retaliation from surviving U.S. forces. . . . We can be sure that the Soviets will use this overwhelming power to their political advantage.

On the conventional level, the Soviets achieved similar superiority. Soviet and Warsaw pact forces now hold European advantages of 3–2 in manpower; 5–1 in tanks; 3–1 in aircraft; and 3–1 in nuclear weapons. The Soviets spend between 11 and 18 percent of GNP on the military; the NATO countries, 4 percent. And because the Soviets have means of compulsion not available to the West, they can maintain this military machine while spending only one-third of their budget on personnel, compared to more than 55 percent in the United States and Europe. The Soviet military buildup continued right through a decade of restraint and negotiation on the part of the U.S.; from 1970 on, the Kremlin spent more than twice what the United States spent on weaponry.

Some of the U.S. gestures to convince the Soviets to stop this buildup stretch credulity.

In 1963, the United States decided to deactivate 2,000 of

its B-47 bombers, 70 B-58 bombers, 185 Atlas and Titan missiles, and 100 Thor and Jupiter missiles. We cut back production of the Titan II missiles by 200. The Soviets retained plans to construct 200 SS-7 and SS-8 missiles and more than 500 SS-4 and SS-5 missiles.

From 1965 to 1967, the U.S. moved to freeze its land missile force at 1,054, and submarine-launched missiles at 656. This would allow the Soviets to achieve equality by 1969, and thus, Secretary McNamara argued, set the stage for arms limitation and reduction talks to move both nations away from nuclear stalemate. In 1969, Richard Nixon took office and the U.S. added plans to scrap more than 250 B-52 bombers.

Yet from 1969 to 1975, the Soviets added more than 800 new fixed missile launchers, developed and began production on the new Backfire bomber, and obtained a refire capability for fixed missile launchers. That refire capability is critical, because the U.S. had long assumed that a SALT limit on launchers would effectively limit total missiles. It is far easier to verify large launchers from space than missiles. And, since neither side was thought to be able to use the same launchers over and over to fire a series of heavy and powerful intercontinental missiles, it looked like a good approach. Soviet refire capability enables the Kremlin to make use of more than 2,000 warheads that the United States thought would be obsolete under the SALT I agreement. Indeed, that refire capacity, along with multiple-warhead missiles, helped throw the whole arms limitation dialogue out of kilter.

The SALT I treaty was signed, and, as it took effect, the U.S. continued to put forth no plans for new missile, bomber, or submarine systems. Yet, between the signing of SALT I and 1978, the Soviets nearly tripled their own counterforce and throw weight capacity. Indeed, from 1977 to 1980, the U.S. canceled production of the B-1 bomber; delayed by four years construction of the MX missile, which we have yet to deploy; slowed construction on the Trident submarine and submarine missiles; deactivated more than 150 Polaris submarine missiles; stopped deployment of 100 Minuteman

III missiles; and surrendered significant technological leads in anti-ballistic missile defense, and in the placing of multiple warheads on the same missile.

From 1974 to 1980, the U.S. canceled more than 700 delivery vehicles, 6,180 warheads, and 10,450 more warheads, assuming future planned cuts in various programs. (All figures from *International Security Review*, Foreign Affairs Council, 1980, pp. 14–22.)

Over these same years, the Soviets deployed two new missile systems. They engaged in wholesale substitution of heavy SS-18 and SS-19 missiles for the lighter SS-16. They added 100 MIRVed warheads per year. They placed four new strategic missile systems under construction. They built more than 200 Backfire bombers along with three newer models, and made a series of significant technical advances in missile accuracy, anti-submarine warfare, and air defense.

The net, as compared with the U.S.'s unilateral reductions, was an addition of more than 1,000 missiles, 500 bombers, and 500 submarine delivery vehicles—more than 6,000 warheads of deadly accuracy and high throw weight, quite capable of knocking out America's lighter, more vulnerable missiles in a disarming first strike. They developed cold launch capabilities to ensure that even a hit by U.S. missiles on Soviet launchers—long thought to be another guarantee linking launcher numbers to missile numbers—could not succeed in keeping Soviet missiles on the ground.

Even so, the question America's MAD strategy imposed on all these numbers is, "So what?" In a world where each side can blow up the other, who cares about an advantage in missiles or bombers? As Henry Kissinger testified at a Senate hearing in 1974, "What in the name of God is strategic superiority? What is the significance of it operationally, politically, militarily. . . . What do you do with it?" The answer, even in a world of MAD strategies, is that strategic superiority is obtained when one side has so much offensive power that it can knock out the other side and its offensive power without fear of significant retaliation—a first strike. Kissinger admitted in 1979: "My[1974] statement reflected fatigue and exasperation, not analysis. If both sides maintain the balance, then, indeed, the arms race is futile and SALT has its place in strengthening stability. But if we opt out of the race unilaterally, we will probably be faced eventually with a younger group of Soviet leaders who will figure out what can be done with strategic superiority." Or, as Richard Nixon wrote, "We have been engaged in SALT for a decade and have practiced strategic arms restraint longer than we have had SALT agreements. The benefits originally expected have not materialized. In fact, our strategic situation has steadily deteriorated. Clearly, our attention should not now be on SALT, but identifying and remedying the weaknesses in our strategic posture."

Nixon's, of course, was not the only administration to enter office pledging U.S. military might to match the Soviet buildup, and to govern more on the basis of unilateral U.S. gestures (many imposed by Congress). And, like other administrations, his would look back at the failure of the U.S. to keep pace. One of the interesting characteristics of postwar history is the degree to which each administration found itself on the same offensive buildup *cum* offensive talks treadmill. Dwight Eisenhower entered office promising a tougher but more hi-tech defense to expand American influence at low cost; he left John Kennedy a military machine of awesome power but little flexibility. Kennedy promised "flexible response" and "pay any price" defenses, but endured humiliation at the Bay of Pigs and bequeathed Lyndon Johnson the Vietnam War. Johnson and Robert McNamara brought forth plans for the first ABM system, but left office urging that the U.S. and the Soviets jointly agree never to deploy one. Richard Nixon warned against the "growing nuclear threat" that Johnson had failed to meet, but left in place the SALT I and ABM treaties and a whole framework of detente.

The period of nuclear weapons and the evolution of MAD strategy, then, has been characterized by a series of lurches— of alternating desires to compete with Soviet buildups and to pacify the Kremlin leadership at arms talks. All of this was a not unlikely response to assured destruction strategy. Over the long haul, Americans were asked to support a series of offensive weapons in order to aim those weapons at Soviet cities. Yet this occured even as they were told that the Soviet leadership was rational and could be dealt with; and that, ultimately, the continuing arms race was irrational and unwinnable by either side.

If we look at the trend of American defense expenditures in the MAD era, expressed as a share of GNP, then all the lurches, stops, and starts smooth out into one, steady, downward-curving trend:

YEARS	DEFENSE AS A PERCENT OF G.N.P.
1953–56 average	10.2
1957–60	8.7
1961–64	8.4
1965–68	8.1
1969–72	7.7
1973–76	5.7
1977–80	5.1

The age of MAD thus coincides neatly with a linear decline in the willingness of the American people to support defense. And why not? The American people weren't paying for a defense. They weren't purchasing a system which could protect them and their families from an aggressor, from the Kremlin or otherwise, once that aggressor chose to attack with the most powerful weapons on earth. Apart from its military flaws, MAD seems to be doctrine guaranteed to undermine whatever political mandate the American people occasionally express for greater defense—a mandate they delivered to Eisenhower, Kennedy, Nixon, and later, Ronald Reagan.

The Reagan administration, in fact, provides a good case study in the difficulty of maintaining public support for increasing military budgets. Ronald Reagan and a Republican Senate were swept into office with a mandate that, however one interpreted its particulars, clearly pointed the way toward an American rearmament program. Reagan and the Republicans ran on a platform calling for "military superiority." They promised to end "the Carter coverup of SALT I and II violations." Reagan outlined a schedule of military spending increases well above those planned by the Carter administration. And Americans told George Gallup and other pollsters that they supported such a program: Better than two-thirds of the country thought defense spending should be increased, according to regular samplings on the subject.

High expectations prevailed, then, as Ronald Reagan took office and set about enacting the military agenda he had proposed in the campaign. Early budget projections called for military spending to rise by better than 5 percent per year even after accounting for inflation, bringing U.S. defense spending back to 7 percent of GNP by the end of Reagan's first term.

The President gave rhetorical emphasis to his support for the American military, too. In a speech at West Point he promised "never again" to subject U.S. fighting men to the humiliation of fighting a half-committed U.S. war effort, as in Vietnam. Military pay increases were granted to bring military salaries closer in line with those of the rest of the country. Morale in the services soared; reenlistment rates shot up 30 percent in six months, and for the first time since the inception of the all-volunteer army, the three services met their recruiting and manpower goals. Two of every three new enlistees, as against one of three in 1980, were high school graduates.

Yet within one year of this auspicious start, the very supporters who had backed Ronald Reagan in his election bid were backing down on their support for his defense policies. Not because the new president had gone too far; rather, because they saw the goal of a revitalized military slipping away, up against a tide of increasing congressional and public pressure to drop the military buildup plan almost before it began. The Committee On the Present Danger issued a report in the fall of 1981 terming the Reagan plan "woefully inadequate." The Heritage Foundation issued an extensive report titled "The Reagan Defense Budget: Failing to Meet the Threat." Had the President and his calls for "mas-

sive defense hikes" squandered public, pro-military senti-
ment in just a few months in office? Hardly. What happened,
instead, was a renewal of the same old public doubts that
have plagued every administration since Harry Truman's.

In fact, in the summer of 1982, as Congress was complet-
ing work on Ronald Reagan's first real budget, the "massive"
Reagan program looked rather modest. A five-year comparison of Reagan spending plans with outgoing Carter spending plans reveals almost no increase at all, assuming that
there will be no further cuts in defense spending between
now and 1985, which is unlikely.

U.S. defense outlays in billions of dollars

YEAR	CARTER PLAN	REAGAN PLAN*
1981	162	156
1982	187	182
1983	212	214
1984	239	243
1985	270	279
TOTAL	1070	1074

*August 1982 figures from Senate Budget Committee

Thus, Ronald Reagan's plan called for his administration
to outspend the Carter administration by $4 billion over five
years—a net increase of 0.4 percent, or less than one ten-
thousandth of GNP.

In August 1982, the Congressional Budget Office did a
revised calculation of Reagan-versus-Carter spending levels
based on the changes in inflation and economic growth that
occurred from the time Carter left office and 1982. The
result: If the former Carter plan is adjusted to economic
events of 1981 and 1982, Jimmy Carter, in a hypothetical
second term, would be spending roughly $10 billion more on
defense than Ronald Reagan.

The point of these comparisons is not to denigrate either
Reagan or Carter. The comparisons do highlight, however,
the rapid dissolution of yet another American buildup plan.
How, and why, has this happened?

There are two possibilities. Either Ronald Reagan, John F.

Kennedy, and Dwight Eisenhower were incompetent leaders, unable to sustain support for their defense plans; or, there is a critical flaw in the American psyche, the U.S. Congress, or our military strategy, that makes it impossible for any president to rally the people behind a military rearmament program that will, perforce, take many years to bring about.

Even suppose Reagan or some future president could ignite, and sustain, public support for a program to revive American strength. Could our defenses be rebuilt along the offense-only lines that have been the basis of American strategy since Eisenhower? Probably not. A quick comparison of U.S. and Soviet construction rates, provided below, illustrates the tremendous Russian advantage in arms production.

THE ARMS RACE AT A GLANCE
(Projected U.S. and Soviet Production Rates, 1983)

	U.S.	USSR
Intercontinental Missiles	8	200
Bombers	4	30
Submarine-launched Missiles	340	3110
Tanks	705	3110
Helicopters	180	725
Small Ship Combatants	3	60
Major Ship Combatants	8	11
Submarines	3	15

(Reproduced by permission of *The Washington Times*)

Given the industrial capacity of the Soviet arms factories, and the sheer momentum of Soviet production workers—workers already trained, systems already under construction, planned supplies of raw materials for the Russian war industry—it is unlikely that even an ambitious string of American spending increases could enable us to catch up with Soviet arms production, let alone pass it and begin to close the current gap. The barriers to that kind of missile-for-missile, tank-for-tank competition are formidable.

To begin with, the Soviets are now the leading arms supplier in the world. According to a U.S. State Department report released August 2, 1982, the Kremlin sold some 74,000 major systems in Asia, Africa, the Middle East, and Latin America over the past decade, as against 44,000 sold by this country. By manufacturing these arms for others, the Soviets have built up a large reserve arms production capacity. This arms machine can be turned solely to Soviet uses in the event that a U.S.-Soviet race should heat up.

Defense Secretary Caspar Weinberger said in the 1981 report *Soviet Military Power,* "The growth of the Soviet armed forces is made possible by the USSR's military production base which continues to grow at the expense of all other components in the Soviet economy. There are 135 major military industrial plants now operating in the Soviet Union with over 40 million square meters in floor space, a 34 percent increase since 1970. In 1980, these plants produced more than 150 different types of weapons systems for Soviet forces and for export to client states and developing countries." A series of five-year estimates demonstrates "the Soviet ability to sustain high rates of production."

Even hints of a new strategy—John Kennedy's "flexible response" approach in 1960, Ronald Reagan's 1983 call for researching the idea of a true defense—have had the effect of significantly buoying congressional and public support for a stronger America. Those gains proved illusory for John Kennedy, and will prove illusory for all future presidents as long as the change in strategy from all-offense to defense remains only a hazy idea to be carried out in the event of a miraculous technological breakthrough. Scarcely had Kennedy's men begun drawing up plans for systems to meet his call for a true defense, then they began imposing impossible demands on those systems before they would consider building them.

Defenses must be capable of thwarting every missile that might land in America; defenses must be unassailable themselves; defensive technologies must be perfected and the systems completely designed before we can or will begin the strategic shift. Imagine if Congress had demanded a missile that would never miss its target; a bomber that could never be shot down; a submarine that the Soviets could never replicate. Had these demands been placed on offensive systems, America might have no Department of Defense at all.

No administration, in short, has made the bold commitment to building defense that it has made to building offense. When one does, it will find a whole array of technologies and systems for protecting the U.S., and the world, from the threat of nuclear holocaust. Systems that we could be building not for Luke Skywalker or Buck Rogers, but for us. A defense that truly defends. Today.

IV

From Space,
A True Defense

CONVENTIONAL WISDOM HAS IT that there can be no defense against nuclear weapons. That a ballistic missile, once in flight, is indestructible. That bombers and submarines cannot be destroyed, at least not if they are armed with strategic weapons. That cities cannot be protected. That civil defense is futile.

To the extent that these presumptions are ever qualified, it is generally only by allowing that defense is a possibility "well into the next century, if ever."

Simple historical and technological perspective ought to suggest that this idea is ludicrous. History records any number of "absolute weapons." In his analysis of the French military defeat in World Wars I and II, Charles de Gaulle notes how French generals first underestimated the effects of the machine gun in World War I, then came to regard it as the "ultimate weapon" in World War II—both errors costing million of French lives. The French failed to see the growing importance of the machine gun, then of the tank and air power as an integral part of the battle. The tank, for its part, has in recent years become increasingly vulnerable to the guided missile—and the guided missile itself to electronic countermeasures. Newtonian physics, trench warfare, and the crossbow all gave way in due time to more sophisticated and effective weaponry. Those who failed to see these eventualities failed to do so at their own risk.

America, if it ignores the growing opportunities of space, electronics, and weapons guidance technology, could make an equally disastrous mistake.

Consider for a moment just what defending against a nuclear missile involves. This, as of now, is the central problem of building an overall defense. We already know how to prevent a bomber from reaching its target, how to sink a submarine, and so on. About 80 percent of the Soviet nuclear arsenal is in the form of missiles. A missile launched at the U.S. moves so fast that if you tossed an ice cube at it and hit it, you would divert it from its course sufficiently to render it impotent. This may sound incredible considering the power of a nuclear warhead, but power no more makes a missile invulnerable than a strong punch can protect a boxer with a glass jaw. Think of a car moving by you at 60 miles an hour. If you toss a pebble onto its windshield as it whizzes by, the glass shatters. In the same way, a nuclear missile's high speed makes it vulnerable.

The problem of tracking a missile, figuring out where to hit it, or firing something at it that will hit it, is not particularly elusive, either. Few question our ability to track down a Soviet jet, moving at speeds similar to a missile and much closer to the ground, emitting as few electronic and other traceable signals as possible. Our ability to hit such jets is unquestioned, as our fighter planes did with ease over Lebanon and Libya in recent years. Once a missile is fired, it moves in a relatively fixed trajectory; it has no human pilot to enable it to dodge, evade, or fire back at hostile attackers. Indeed, while a strategic missile is in flight, before it hits its target, it is one of the most easily attacked weapons imaginable. It has all the mobility and counterpunch ability of a dinosaur.

The real feasibility or infeasibility of a defense against nuclear weapons hinges on the system as a whole. If the Soviets can launch all of their missiles, how many can we knock down in space? How man can we shoot down using ground-based ABMs? How many would leak through? What might we do to protect our cities from missiles that do leak through? The answers to these and similar questions will give us a rough idea of what a defense system could and could not accomplish, but even then we will be left with the fundamental question of what we expect a defense to do. Should it guarantee that 90 percent of our population would survive such a war? Eighty percent? Fifty? Would a defense be adequate if it provided no rock-bottom guarantees at all—but did throw so much uncertainty into the calculations of someone contemplating an attack on the U.S. that they would have to decide not to, because our surviving conventional forces and population, and the bitterness of world opinion, would rise up and destroy them?

In order for proposals to defend against nuclear weapons to have any meaning, we must begin to think about nuclear weapons in an entirely different way than we are used to thinking about them. We must decide whether saving 100 million, 150 million, or 250 million lives has any military, human, or moral significance. We must, on the one hand, stop thinking in the doomsday terms of all-or-nothing defense, and be willing to consider one system that might save 10 million lives, another that might save five million, another that might protect Chicago, another that might protect Los Angeles.

We must, on the other hand, ask ourselves in cold, rational terms what a nuclear war would mean to America and the Soviet Union today with no defenses. We must, in the final analysis, view the choice not in terms of the next system to be built, or the next arms treaty to be concluded, but as a choice between two diverging paths. The path to defense is filled with questions, but so is the path of offense and arms control: What if the Soviets cheat? What if they don't, and each side manages to freeze forever at its current level of destructive power—could this situation be maintained continually with both sides choosing never to strike? What if we eliminate all nuclear arms from the Soviet Union and the United States, only to have a Third World power construct ten bombs and blackmail the rest of the world?

Only if we take the long view can we choose wisely between two paths—to make a choice based not on what dangers present themselves in the first few steps down each path, but, rather, where we can reasonably expect the paths to end.

As we compare different military strategies, then, we

ought to view them over time. MAD is not just a theory for how we avoid nuclear war today. It is an orientation toward nuclear weapons for tomorrow, and several years down the line. In the same way, strategic defense—an alternative to MAD—is a series of steps. There are immediate defensive options that would radically improve our position even in the short run. There are others, farther down the road, that would end our reliance on the threat of assured destruction altogether. The minute we take this view, we begin to see that defense presents many immediately available options. Precisely because America has turned away from defense for decades, even small increments of defense would dramatically increase our security in the short term, much as if one added even a rickety third leg to a two-legged stool.

In 1980, a group—Project High Frontier—was formed under the auspices of the Heritage Foundation to examine just what might be done to immediately defend the U.S. The project's findings are best set forth by the report filed March 5, 1982, in *The Washington Post.*

"A new study, sponsored by the conservative Heritage Foundation, proposes a major shift in U.S. defense strategy in which non-nuclear . . . satellites in space would destroy Soviet missiles as they are flying towards the United States," the *Post's* Michael Getler wrote.

"The study, which has been submitted to the Reagan administration, envisions a crash program to make a technological end run around the growing Soviet missile threat that would 'nullify or substantially reduce it.' It would take advantage of the U.S. edge in space technology, *use equipment already in development,* not require any new American weapons, and is not based on attacking missile silos in the Soviet Union." (Emphasis added.)

One reason Getler's description of the strategic defense issue is so apt is that it captures most, though not all, of the broad range of actions which must be undertaken in concert if the shift to defense is to be made. There are technical actions involving particular systems—though the High Frontier report was quick to point out that its technical recommendations were only illustrative; that is, meant to show simply that it is plausible, using current technology, to design a defense. There are strategic actions to reorient the Pentagon from its MAD posture that stresses offense, to a new set of priorities, including defense. There is the possibility of a different approach to arms competition, shifting away from a missile-for-missile, production-based race to an emphasis on defense and technology—an "end run," as Getler put it. There must be a new approach to buying weapons that allows some systems—such as a strategic defense—to be built with a high-priority, Manhattan Project-style approach. There is a need for political emphasis on the new strategy and its immediate possibilities, a new involvement of the American people in forming strategy that did not exist when MAD was forming. What is required is a new geopolitical emphasis on space, the emerging high ground of economic and military strength and the natural basing mode for a strategic defense.

So, just as it is important to view defense as a wholly different approach to the arms race, and not just a technical decision over weapons, so is it important to understand that the shift to defense will involve a package of actions. Remove one of the parts and you lose the whole.

If the President called for a space-based missile defense, for example, but tried to do it under the old strategy of MAD, he would find little rationale for advancing his new system. If he tried to make the change in strategy without involving the people to a degree not seen in the MAD era, he would quickly find support dissipating. If America sought to build a defense through business-as-usual procedures, we would find that it takes 15 to 20 years to get a proposed new system through the Congress, past all the critics, and out in the field. Hence, unless a prior decision is made by the country to put a small number of vital systems on a fast track, that defense might never be deployed until it is already obsolete. This is a problem that one does not face when designing a bullet, because the human body changes very little; it is an enormous difficulty the closer you move to the cutting edge of U.S.-Soviet competition: high technology.

The problem of American military inferiority is really a number of problems stemming from bad strategy. Any attempt to attack them piecemeal—without at least considering the relationship of the parts—will fail. This point will become more important when we analyze some of the attacks on the idea of a strategic defense, because so many of those attacks focus on one defense recommendation without taking into account the others. A critic looking at cost estimates for a defense, for example, might find the time and cost estimated to build the system unrealistically low—unless he took into account the fact that defense advocates support a wholly different method of acquiring important systems. A skeptic of the civil defense program might consider the recommendations impractical—unless he realized that defense advocates see civil defense as just the final tier of a multi-layered defense system of satellites, point and ABM defenses, air defense and submarine warfare tactics, and so on; as a kind of mop-up effort, in other words, to limit the harm any hostile missile might do if it managed to leak through a whole series of systems designed to shoot it down.

Viewing the problem of defense from these two vantage points, with a realization that no defense is perfect, and that no defense is possible without a broad program of action, it becomes clear that none of the individual options for achieving defense are satisfactory in and of themselves. Taken together, however, they form an attractive menu for U.S. strategy makers in the 1980s.

POINT DEFENSES

One goal of an emerging U.S. strategy of defense could be to protect existing American nuclear weapons. Until now, the problem of maintaining a sufficient deterrent force has been attacked simply by building more weapons of our own. If the Soviets add 10 missiles, we must thus add several missiles of our own to prevent their offensive force from overwhelming ours in a first strike.

Point defenses emerged as a serious object of consideration in the Pentagon many years ago when the search for less expensive alternatives to ABM (anti-ballistic missile) area defenses was still an active concern. Generally, an ABM aims to defend a large area; in the case of the ABMs envisioned by the 1972 U.S.-Soviet treaty, an area as large as the city of Moscow. Such defenses naturally involve many radars, sophisticated guided intercept missiles capable of knocking out an incoming missile many miles from its target, and so on. Point defenses concentrate on defending a small, well-defined area, and thus involve less sophistication and fewer radars.

One system, the swarmjet point defense, has already been tested by the U.S. and found highly workable. Swarmjet, or similar point defenses, deployed around even a handful of our existing deterrent forces, would almost immediately eliminate the short-term Soviet threat to American missiles. At a cost of $2 billion, for example, the U.S. could protect the MX missile in existing Minuteman silos in North Dakota, as compared to costs of $10 billion to $40 billion for deploying the MX in a concrete-intensive "dense pack" scheme, or $60 billion and more for Jimmy Carter's racetrack plan.

Should the U.S. begin to concentrate on active defense systems like swarmjet, several things would happen. First, the need to build more offensive weapons in the short term—while we are still reliant on a MAD strategy—would be substantially reduced. This would be an incentive for Soviet flexibility at arms control negotiations, since for every missile the Soviets might build, the U.S. could add several new swarmjet rockets to its defense system at a far smaller expense. The arms race, pitting expensive heavy missiles against small, cheap intercept vehicles, thus becomes an extremely expensive proposition for the Kremlin.

Most important, the shift to a swarmjet defense would be the first step toward a broader population defense should arms negotiations continue to come up empty in the coming years. Placed around civil defense centers, for example, swarmjet would be a cheap and effective alternative to the ABM schemes thought necessary in the 1960s to provide general protection for our cities.

How would a point defense system work? For a layman's understanding, the swarmjet defense involves three main components: (1) A radar system, located 10,000 to 20,000 feet in front of existing Minuteman silos, which detects, tracks, and is used to calculate an intercept point for incoming missiles; (2) a launcher system for swarmjet rockets,

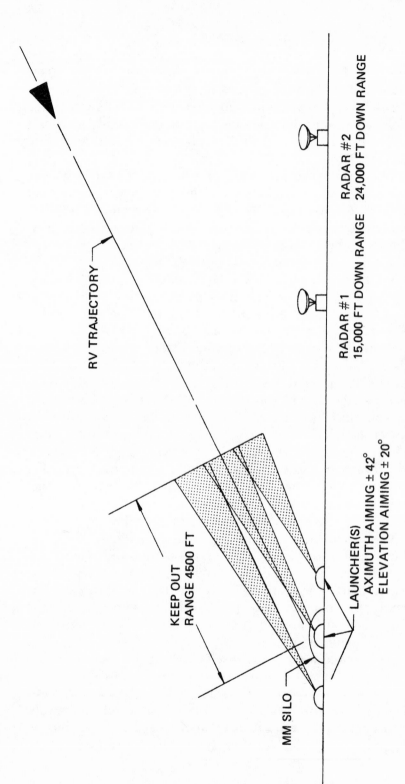

Figure 1. Swarmjet Engagement Schematic (Courtesy of High Frontier)

hardened to protect itself against a one-megaton blast 3,000 feet away; the launchers aim and fire swarmjet rockets in one-second bursts; and (3) the swarmjet rockets themselves, a cluster of conventional projectiles that fly out to knock out an attacking missile. Again, because nuclear reentry vehicles travel at such high speeds, the kinetic energy of a single one of this "swarm" of rockets would be sufficient to kill the attacking warhead and protect our missiles. (See figure 1.)

Other options for point defense systems might include the Low Altitude Defense System, or LOADS, under development by several private companies including T.R.W. and McDonnel-Douglas, the Limited Area ABM under study by Vought Corporation, and a similar system designed by Sandia National Laboratories at Albuquerque. Because the U.S. has spurned defensive options for so many years, production and deployment of one of these basic point defenses would represent a major step forward. Many of the problems likely to be encountered by other defensive systems, whether on ground or space, will be encountered in the construction of a point defense for protection of our deterrent. Smoothing out the bugs for such systems now, and enhancing our deterrent quickly and cheaply, we can then move forward with plans for a more complete defense.

As it is, the Pentagon and the Congress have almost ignored the point defense option, an option that makes sense even under MAD strategic formulas.

GLOBAL BASED MISSILE DEFENSES

Ground-based systems are very efficient at protecting a small, well-defined area such as an ICBM silo or civil defense shelter. They do not, however, provide an efficient means for defending a whole city, state, or continent from weapons of mass destruction. One of the reasons the defense option was rejected by McNamara is that most analyses of missile defense at the time looked at the problem from the ground up. The U.S. had launched a space program, yes, but had yet to think along the lines of a space shuttle and other programs designed to cut the cost of transporting materials into space.

Hence, space was not actively considered as a possible base for missile defenses. And the problems of ground defense

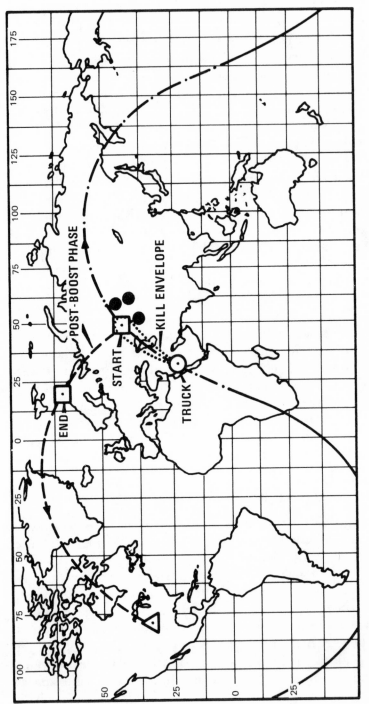

Figure 2. Cross-Track Intercept Example: Satellite Defense
(Courtesy of High Frontier)

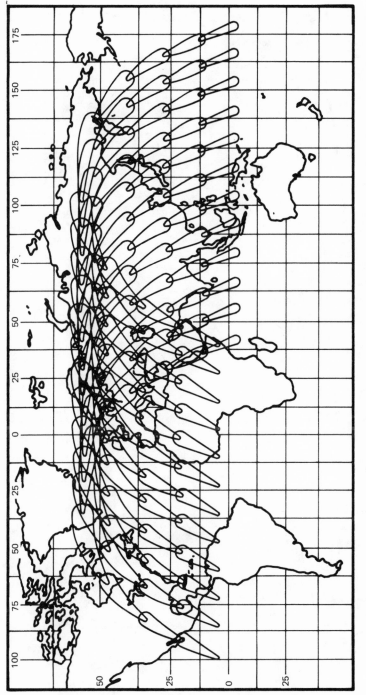

Figure 3. Example Footprints (½ Northern Hemisphere): Satellite
Defense (Courtesy of High Frontier)

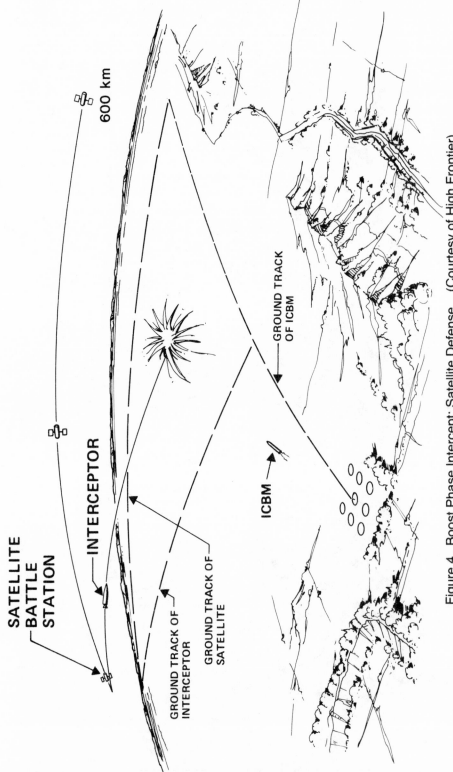

SATELLITE BATTLE STATION

600 km

INTERCEPTOR

GROUND TRACK OF INTERCEPTOR

GROUND TRACK OF SATELLITE

GROUND TRACK OF ICBM

ICBM

Figure 4. Boost Phase Intercept: Satellite Defense (Courtesy of High Frontier)

were severe. Thousands of ABM systems would have to be built in order to protect large populations. Those ground systems must intercept an ICBM during the final phase of its trajectory, as it zooms down from above. They are vulnerable to deception, liable to be forced to waste their rockets on decoy attack vehicles. They must operate in a severe nuclear environment.

By contrast, a nuclear defense based in space can be flexible, employ simpler technology, and be obtained at relatively low cost. A defense system based in space has the advantage of scanning down on the missiles. It can cover a narrow window of attack through which Soviet missiles would travel as they leave their silos on the way to the U.S., Europe, or Japan. Within five years, at a cost of $12 billion, the United States could deploy a two-layered fleet of satellites that would filter out 98 percent of a Soviet missile launch.

Few scientists doubt the sheer technical possibility of designing a satellite that can track down and hit a missile. Indeed, we already have most of the components. We can trace a missile using its heat path; we can compute where it will travel; we can hit it with any of a number of conventional vehicles that we now use to hit missiles and jets from the ground or the sky.

The system illustrated in figures 2, 3, and 4 is one version of how a satellite defense might work. A large network of satellites, or trucks (figure 2), moves in circular orbits approximately 250–350 nautical miles above the earth. These satellites, 300 or more, move together in spread orbits (figure 3) to form a continuous blanket over Soviet missile fields. Each individual satellite contains enough self-propelled rockets to destroy 50 or more missiles.

In the event of Soviet attack, satellites moving over the launch area track the trajectory of individual missiles at optical wavelengths using the earth's surface as a background. Because the trucks are in independent communication with one another, there is no need to wait for complicated targeting communications between the satellites and earth. U.S. satellites quickly target Soviet missiles and dispatch a rocket to meet them. Such an intercept is shown in figure 4.

Many of the schemes for missile defense discussed to date involve sophisticated laser and particle beam weaponry. Such weapons may indeed become practicable in the near future. But the fact that more perfect systems may come along should not deter us from building imperfect devices now. When man invented the wheel, he didn't wait 2,000 years for the internal combustion engine to come along to build carts and wagons to get him around, while the automobile and the locomotive still lurked far off in the future. By the same token, as scientist Edward Teller told *Time* magazine, "It makes sense to start off with a crude defense now," until even better defenses come along.

A simple, first generation defense, for example, will enable us to solve many of the technical problems that a laser or particle beam system would face also. A concerted drive to reduce the cost of space transport, for instance, would make our first system cheaper—but it would do the same for lasers. As we build a first generation defense we could be devising methods to overcome Soviet attacks on the system. And when the more sophisticated space defenses come along— adherents usually envision a network of 20 or 30 particle beam weapons—they would be protected by a fleet of hundreds of more expendable crafts already in orbit. Finally, deploying a simpler system in the short run would turn our space sector into a true industry. Satellites, particularly military satellites, are, by and large, hand-crafted. Mass production would bring economies of scale and drive down the unit costs of satellite production so that future additions to the defense system—say, laser and particle beam weapons— could be made at a very reasonable cost.

Many of the requirements for a future laser defense can be met as we deploy earlier, simpler systems. One current stumbling block to a defense in space is the high cost, even with the shuttle, of transport. Another is the need for hardened launcher pads that can be used over and over again. Thus, space-based defenses need not be held back as we wait for exotic technologies to be perfected. When they are, the other problems associated with a strategy of defense will have been solved.

LASERS AND PARTICLE BEAM WEAPONRY

It is hard to over-stress the point that a viable U.S. defense system *need not wait* for the kinds of weapons typically pictured in popular magazines and television programs: Star Wars crafts zooming about the galaxy zapping missiles and each other and entire planets. All the requirements for a layered defense can be met without such hi-tech break-throughs, and it would not be prudent to base our security on the prospect that such weapons will become available in the near future.

Nevertheless, there is no doubt that such technologies will be developed someday, or that they would provide an ex-tremely effective defense. Furthermore, such a break-through by either the U.S. or the Soviet Union, while unlikely, could produce a dramatic tilt in the balance of power. The United States should continue and significantly increase its research into advanced technology defenses.

Generally, when we talk about such systems, we are talking about directed energy technologies: high energy lasers, par-ticle beams, high power microwaves, electromagnetic pulse, and others. All involve the generation of intense electromag-netic energy (radio frequencies, X-rays, e.g.) or of small, atomic or sub-atomic particles (electrons, ions, protons). The resulting beam of energy can be directed at targets within or outside the atmosphere with devastating potential.

Beam weapons would provide a superior defense in sev-eral ways. They can be effective at extremely long ranges with, if properly directed, deadly accuracy. They thus would be able to cover a far broader geographical area than early, conventional systems and could defend against a wider array of weaponry. Used in space, such weapons would offer the potential for instantaneous power projection. They could strike against satellites, bombers, intercontinental missiles, submarine and cruise missiles, and even surface targets.

Since such weapons would fire and hit their targets at near the speed of light, evasion becomes extremely difficult. How-ever, laser technologies cannot provide the ultimate weapon any more than nuclear technologies. Evading their destruc-tive power would probably involve methods of confusing their targeting electronically, or shooting them down with equally devastating weapons. A switch to laser technology does mean that the weapons of mass destruction now stock-piled in the U.S. and the Soviet Union would become of little value. Directed energy weapons would be able to rapidly hit one target and then engage another in short periods of time; the only "ammunition" to be reloaded is the energy that they would generate more or less continuously.

This is not the place to evaluate all the gaps in current knowledge that must be filled before such schemes become reality. All the beam technologies require massive amounts of energy not yet obtained in ground experiments; the huge generators needed to produce such beams would cost billions to transport into space. Laser beams suffer from their vulnerability to inclement weather and dust; particle beams are relatively immune to atmospheric disturbances, but require even larger energy platforms and have a shorter range. Laser, microwave, particle beam, and magnetic pulse weapons are far off—but not so far off that the U.S. should not consciously gear its defense programs today to take advantage of these systems of tomorrow.

MANNED SPACE VEHICLES

As a concomitant to the global-based missile defense, the United States should deploy a mobile, high performance spaceplane. The spaceplane would serve a number of missions: inspection and maintenance of U.S. satellites; placing new satellites in correct orbit and correcting faulty orbits of existing satellites; replacing, supplementing, and filling in for unmanned satellites; and, eventually, conducting an active defense of U.S. installations in space.

For all their virtues, current and proposed spacecraft cannot perform some of the useful functions served by a mobile vehicle in space—particularly one that does not have to return to earth. Manned spacecraft programs in the past have generally been aimed either at political objectives (e.g., placing a man on the moon before the Russians) or toward short-run economic goals (performing this-or-that experiment in space for private industry). Hence, manned spacecraft programs and concepts continue to be characterized by dependence on ground support, high operating costs, and low maneuverability.

Current manned spacecraft programs tend to rely on extensive ground tracking and support monitoring, tracking, control, and communication. Because a launch begins each mission, they are costly. A rainstorm can delay a launch for hours or days at a cost of millions of dollars. Once launched, the crafts move with severely limited mobility. At both ends—the craft itself in space, and the fixed control center on the ground—the entire operation is vulnerable.

Our manned flights also take place only for days at a time. A permanent manned presence in space would balance the country's present reliance on unmanned vehicles much as the addition of defensive systems would balance its reliance on offense alone in the nuclear field. Unmanned satellites cannot think, and, at present, can serve only a single mission. They are vulnerable, dependent on earth support, and immobile. A manned spaceplane suffers none of these disadvantages. It ought to be deployed on its own merits, even if the rest of the recommendations for nuclear defense are ignored.

Figure 5 shows one possible design for the spaceplane. The vehicle shown is in the conical shape of ballistic missile reentry vehicles, for easy return to Earth. The proposed craft would carry one pilot and weigh approximately three tons. A storable propellant allows for propulsion in low-to-medium orbits. The system is similar to the range extension provided for conventional aircraft by wing or belly tanks. The engine comprises a ring of small thrusters at the rear of the vehicle. This nonconventional engine is called a plug-cluster and is capable of operating at all altitudes, from sea level to the vacuum of space. The airframe would be made of a non-metal, composite material to achieve lightness, and the entire plane would be covered with lightweight tiles for thermal protection during launch and recovery, similar to those now found on the space shuttle.

CIVIL DEFENSE

Under the doctrine of Mutual Assured Destruction, this nation's citizens remain unprotected hostages to the Soviet Union's steadily growing nuclear strike force. By contrast, the Soviet Union has taken substantial steps to preserve its population in a nuclear war. An effective civil defense program could do much even now to reduce the Soviet threat in a time of crisis. In combination with a global based missile defense, comprehensive anti-bomber defenses, and anti-

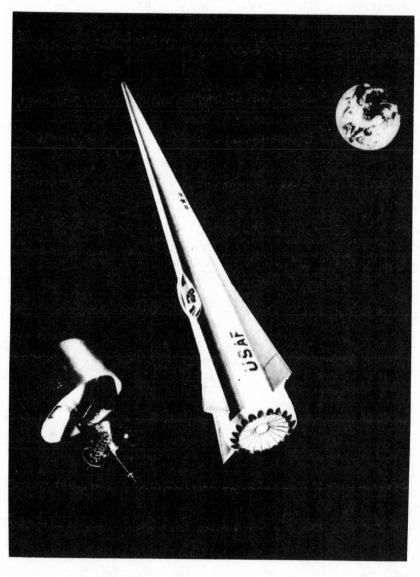

Figure 5. Military High Performance Spaceplane (Courtesy of High Frontier)

submarine warfare, civil defense becomes particularly attractive.

As early as the 1950s, before the Soviets had even deployed any offensive nuclear missiles, the Kremlin initiated an extensive civil defense program that included fallout shelters, planned evacuation of cities, storage of grain and other food, and required survival training for Soviet citizens. In 1961, civil defense was transferred from civilian to military control under Marshal Chuikov. In 1972, civil defense was further elevated in overall Soviet planning, and General A. T. Altunin was appointed commander of the civil defense program with greatly expanded responsibilities.

This alone should tell us something about the Soviet view of MAD—and provide sufficient reason for the U.S. government to scrap the doctrine that decrees that American lives should not be protected through civil defense. Soviet planners regard civil defense as "a strategic factor" that will make a "major contribution toward victory," as the Soviet government stated in a policy paper, "The Philosophical Heritage of V. I. Lenin and Problems of Contemporary War," edited by General Major A. S. Milovidov.

In the next few years, before active defense weapons can be perfected and deployed, American lives can be protected best by rapidly creating a strategically significant, yet relatively cheap, civil defense system—the first step toward Assured Survival. The key to initiating a meaningful civil defense program is credibility: credibility to the Soviet Union, to other hostile nations, to our allies, and above all to a majority of Americans. Credibility will depend on the seriousness of our leaders and the existence of serious plans capable of saving a large number of lives during both an attack and the following recovery period. To receive serious attention and continuing support, civil defense programs must be widely recognized as making an important contribution to the prevention of war. American leaders must stress the positive, hopeful advantages of serious preparations—a stress that will become more credible in the context of a broader, explicit commitment to nuclear defense.

The fiscal year 1982 budget contained funding of about $128 million for civil defense, about 60 cents per capita. In constant dollars, the country is spending less on civil defense today than in 1962.

Worse, the responsibility for civil defense planning now rests with the Federal Emergency Management Agency (FEMA), a catch-all disaster and hazard reduction agency created by President Carter. Whatever its merits, the agency lacks close contact with the Department of Defense, the ability to concentrate on war and survival problems, and engineers schooled in the problems of disaster management under wartime conditions. The agency continues to stockpile outdated and even life-endangering survival instructions for distribution in a crisis. Furthermore, it has avoided many of the hard problems and inevitable controversies generated by realistic civil defense planning, preferring to concentrate on less disputed programs.

An alternative, committed approach to civil defense was provided by President Carter in Presidential Directive 41, "U.S. Civil Defense Policy," on September 29, 1978. The plan, "Program D," called for crisis relocation planning and training, shelter equipment, and up to seven million additional sets of radiation monitoring instruments. Relocation planning would enable some 80 percent of Americans to survive a large scale attack in the mid-1980s, *independent* of any active defense systems—provided that risk area populations are evacuated quickly, that fallout protection has been developed, and that crisis followup actions, like stockpiling, are completed.

On March 30, 1981, FEMA issued a paper on the implementation of Carter's plan and the estimated costs for the program. The paper called for a seven-year program with costs largely deferred until the final three years. If the final three-year push were implemented now, and certain additions made to the program, the United States could achieve modest civil defense progress almost immediately, and complete a significant program by 1985. Besides increased attention from political and civil leaders, which would cost nothing, a number of actions should be taken to supplement Program D:

–Self-help civil defense should be strongly advocated and taught by our official civil defense organizations. An example of the effectiveness of self-help is provided by the Oak Ridge Laboratory's report, *Nuclear War Survival Skills,* a guide, based on realistic field tests with families in several states, to help people unfamiliar with the effects of radiation improve their chances for surviving a nuclear war. Tens of thousands of privately reproduced copies of the pamphlet are currently being used to instruct in the building of fallout shelters and the construction of ventilating pumps, fallout meters, and other homemade life support equipment. Millions of lives could be saved by wide dissemination of this and similar literature.

—Major food reserve programs should be enacted. No civil defense program is meaningful without provision for emergency supplies of food. Provision of basic foods, especially powdered milk for infants, wheat, and bulgar (debranned wheat that has been cooked and redried), will assure urban evacuees that they will not go hungry if plans to redirect normal food deliveries come unglued. President Kennedy recommended in 1961, without success, that some 126 million bushels of wheat be stored in 191 metropolitan areas. A bushel of wheat will provide an austere but health-maintaining diet for an adult for one month. The cost of a one-month supply of baby food should come to no more than $18 per infant; of basic foodstuffs for adults, about $15 per person. Such stockpiling could save millions of lives, and would add greatly to the credibility of American civil defense plans.

—Blast shelters, to protect policemen, firemen, and other essential workers, should be mass produced. They could be installed below ground in parks and other open spaces, well removed from buildings and from the worst dangers of fire and carbon monoxide. (Thousands of Japanese at Hiroshima, and some 135,000 Germans at Dresden, were trapped in shelters under buildings or died of carbon monoxide poisoning.) Using reinforced basements, as currently advocated by FEMA, would be disastrous. A corrugated steel blast shelter designed for mass production has been developed and successfully tested at 50 pounds pressure per square inch in a nuclear test at White Sands, New Mexico. This shelter can be manufactured, delivered, installed, and equipped at a cost of less than $200 per person to be protected. Surveys show that 100,000 blast shelter spaces are needed to cover 200,000 policemen, firemen, and doctors working around the clock in 12-hour shifts. Thus, the required blast shelters would cost less than $200 million in 1982 dollars.

–Blast-tested designs of blast shelters, along with description and explanation, should be made readily available to the public. Concerned urban citizens are unlikely to give their support to a civil defense effort unless it provides them with a hope for survival.

–Individual communities should develop their own detailed plans for the rapid construction of shelters and life support equipment during crises of different durations. Such plans should include designs of both expedient shelters for a rapidly escalating crisis and of permanent blast shelters for possible construction during a prolonged, recognized crisis. Local contractors should receive training and be listed together with local sources of earthmoving machines and shelter building materials.

Athens, Tennessee, a town of about 35,000 people, with few buildings affording good fallout protection, has developed just such a plan. Athens is prepared to build covered trench shelters for all its citizens in two days' time. However Strangelovian such schemes may sound, they could save millions of lives.

The seven million sets of radiation-monitoring instruments envisioned by Program D should be produced in an accelerated two-year program. These essential instruments could be stockpiled outside of likely U.S. target areas, ready for distribution during a crisis. With such instruments, millions of citizens would be able to determine the changing radiation dose rates that could be endangering them.

The total cost of Program D, with the suggested modifications, is estimated at $4.5 billion. This total includes the $2.6 billion estimated by FEMA for Program D, about $1.6 billion for a one-month austere food supply stored in hot areas for 110 million adult and infant evacuees, and roughly $200 million for blast shelters for essential workers needed in high risk areas.

The total annual cost would amount to less than $7 for every American. It would put U.S. per capita civil defense spending in the general range of the Scandinavian countries ($9 per citizen) but still well below the $32 per capita spent in Switzerland, and only at the bottom range of Soviet expenditures, estimated to fall somewhere between $8 and $20 a year. Once this realistic war-surviving project is underway, it will signal that the U.S. has abandoned Mutual Assured Destruction and is determined to attain Assured Survival.

THE RESULT: A LAYERED DEFENSE

The programs described have merit individually, but it is important to remember that they are most effective implemented together. In the case of a strategic defense, the sum of the parts is greater than the whole.

For example, one of the critical elements for carrying out a civil defense program is public acceptance. In the absence of any visible commitment to defense as a strategy, civil defense programs to date have floundered, been ridiculed as a bizarre and futile effort against the horrific carnage of nuclear war. Yet, a broad-based commitment to active defenses—the High Frontier basic technology satellites, ground-based point defense, and further research into laser and particle beam warfare—erases that element of incredibility from the debate over civil defense, by providing a plausible shield against attack. Once we need worry about only the few missiles or bombs that may leak through our active defenses in space and on the ground, civil defense becomes a workable proposition. Our layered defense thereby enhances the likelihood of public acceptance and cooperation.

Another synergism involves two layers apart from civil defense: active defenses in space on the one hand, and active defenses on the ground, on the other. Even a well-conceived ground-based defense rests on a fixed number of radars and intercept launchers. And while ground-based defenses alone multiply the number of missiles the Soviets need to achieve a first strike, their construction still presents Kremlin planners with a relatively straightforward arithmetic problem. For each anti-missile station the U.S. adds, the Kremlin knows, it must construct two to four missiles in order to knock out that station. This is not a problem to be shrugged away. Provided simple technologies are used, the U.S. can build new ABM stations for less than the Soviets can build four new missiles to knock it out.

Adding two layers of space-based satellites to America's defenses turns the arithmetic problem into a complicated exercise in calculus. Several new variables enter into the equation. Some Soviet missiles may make it past the first layer of space defenses but be knocked out by the second. Others may be netted by the point defense. Some missiles that make it through all three nets will miss their target. And no one knows which missiles will be stopped where in advance, which multiplies by a factor of five to ten the number of missiles the Soviets must launch in order to make certain of hitting a given target.

Far more detailed descriptions and analyses of these and similar possibilities for defense are available.[1] The purpose of this chapter is not to describe how each might be built, how it would overcome every possible objection, how in combination they could guarantee no nuclear war fatalities. The purpose has been to outline a group of systems that would drastically complicate any attacker's plans, shift future arms competition from increasingly threatening technologies to defensive ones, and, in the process, save millions of lives should Soviet leaders in the Kremlin ever do the unthinkable.

---

[1] Additional sources:

1. Daniel O. Graham, et. al., *High Frontier: A New National Strategy* (Washington, DC: The Heritage Foundation, 1982). Now published by Project High Frontier, 1010 Vermont Avenue, N.W., Washington, DC 20005.

2. Thomas Karas, *The New High Ground: Systems and Weapons of Space-Age War* (New York: Simon and Schuster, 1983).

3. *Project Defender,* U.S. Department of Defense, 1963.

4. *Soviet Military Power,* U.S. Department of Defense, 1981.

V

Defending the Frontier

OCTOBER 4, 1957. More than a quarter century ago, the Soviet Union fired into a space a 184-pound ball of machinery. Called Sputnik 1, it was the world's first artificial satellite. More important, it was the first step in a race to exploit the potential of space—a race that may determine which of two countries, the U.S. or the Soviet Union, will shape the world to come.

Space is the natural basing mode for a new generation of weapons to defend the United States from nuclear attack. Creating a defense that defends, therefore, has significant implications for this competition. It will strike many Americans as puzzling even to hear that this competiton continues—wasn't it settled, after all, on the night in 1969 when two Americans, Neil Armstrong and Buzz Aldrin, set foot on the moon? But the moon landing, while exhilarating and psychologically important, was only a symbolic victory. The battle for space will turn more on this country's ability to harness the economic potential of outer space than on winning a sprint to any individual achievement. It was an Italian explorer sailing under Spanish flag who crossed the Atlantic to the New World. It was largely the British, though, who colonized these new continents, built a powerful merchant fleet and military armada, and established a benevolent *Pax Britannicus* that expanded world trade, spread Western culture, and made England the major power in world affairs.

Americans have always been good on frontiers, but today we face a challenge that will demand more than just resources and crash programs. It is a long-term challenge that will test our geopolitical insight: Can we establish, and meet, goals that will necessarily be, not three months or five years, but perhaps decades in the meeting? It is a challenge that will test our commitments to peace and strength: Can we resolve to defend our assets in space—which even now are threatened—and at the same time remain committed to a course that will leave space, like the high seas, open for traffic and commerce to all nations?

In the more than 25 years since Sputnik was launched, the United States, rather like the Aesopian hare, has dashed forward with spectacular inventiveness and courage whenever its resolve to move was mustered. Meanwhile, the Soviet Union—the tortoise—has plodded steadily onward. The U.S. Defense Department's 1981 book, *Soviet Military Power,* describes the Russian program:

> The Soviets have a vigorous and constantly expanding military space program. In the past ten years, they have been launching spacecraft at over 75 per year, at the rate of four-to-five times that of the United States. The annual payload weight placed into orbit by the Soviets is even more impressive— 660,000 pounds, or ten times that of the United States. Some, but by no means all, of this differential can be accounted for by long-life U.S. satellites using miniaturized high technology components. Such an activity rate is expensive to underwrite, yet the Soviets are willing to expend resources on space hardware at an approximate 8 percent per year growth rate in constant dollars.
>
> We estimate that 70 percent of Soviet space systems serve a purely military role, another 15 percent serve dual military-civil roles, and the remaining 15 percent are purely civil.
>
> The Soviets appear to be interested in and possibly developing an improved [anti-satellite weapon]. A very large space booster similar in performance to the Apollo program's Saturn V is under development and will have the capability to launch very heavy payloads into orbit, including even larger and more capable laser weapons. This booster is estimated to have six to seven times the launch weight capability of the

space shuttle. . . . The new booster will be capable of putting very large permanently manned space stations into orbit. The Soviet goal of having continuously manned space stations may support both defensive and offensive weapons in space with man in the space station for target selection, repairs and adjustments and positive command and control. The Soviets' predominently military space program is expected to continue to produce steady gains in reliability, sophistication, and operational capability.

After a brief flurry of activity in the mid- to late '60s, the U.S. space efforts have steadily declined while the Soviet Union's have grown substantially, prompting Dartmouth professor Robert Jastrow, founder and former director of the NASA Goddard Institute for Space Studies, to write, "Persuasive evidence has begun to emerge convincing me that the Soviet Union is once again gaining the lead in what may turn out to be the most critical area of space activity: its utilization for military purposes." (*New York Times Magazine*, October 3, 1982). Far more important, after all, than who is "ahead" or "behind" in this overall race, is who can do what: which side can achieve what in space, who can protect his assets.

The Soviets have never made any bones about it: They see space as just another theatre for the final triumph of Marxism over the West—a triumph, moreover, presented largely in military terms. On the day Sputnik was launched, *Pravda,* the official voice of the Soviet Communist Party, editorialized: "The launching of the Sputnik is a victory of Soviet man who, with Bolshevist boldness and clearness of purpose, determination, and energy knows how to move forward. It has again been proved convincingly and vividly that the Soviet socialist system is the best form for the organization of workers free of the shackles of exploitation." A few days later, Soviet chief of state Nikita Khrushchev pointed out that the same rocket capability that enabled the Soviets to put a satellite in space could also be used to fire a missile at the United States. Simply "attach a hydrogen warhead" and you had the intercontinental missile, the ICBM.

Russia's steady, foresighted commitment to space—about

$20 billion a year versus $13 billion for the U.S.—is starting to bear fruit. The first Soviet strategy, it appears, has been to develop a substantial anti-satellite capability.

The Kremlin began its anti-satellite warfare program around 1966, just as American satellite launches were reaching their peak. Since then the Soviets have conducted several hundred tests on a broad arsenal of possible satellite weapons. The most common method involves use of a standard missile that zooms directly from its launch pad to the targeted satellite. Some are designed to catch up to and destroy their target within several orbits. Others act as mines in space, floating near an operating U.S. satellite on apparently independent missions of their own, but rigged with explosives that could be detonated to kill our satellite whenever the Soviets choose.

In November 1982, David Hoffman of *The Washington Times* reported that U.S. intelligence experts believed the Soviets had conducted 11 tests of this simple kill method, seven of which were successful. *The Wall Street Journal* later estimated 10 hits in 20 attempts for all of 1982. Either figure is impressive; a 50 percent success rate of firing cheap missiles at expensive satellites is quite respectable. The Soviets continue to research and test methods that would be still quicker and more accurate. They have spent roughly five times more money than the U.S. on laser and particle beam weaponry. U.S. intelligence officials say the Soviets may deploy a space-based laser within one to five years. (*The New York Times*, October 18, 1982.) Given the state of Soviet technology, it would probably lack the power to serve as an anti-missile defense, although it would, however, extend Soviet anti-satellite capabilities far beyond their present range. Soviet ground-launched weapons have proved accurate (so far) only against lower-altitude satellites, leaving many more valuable U.S. assets, such as the higher-altitude early warning satellites that might alert us to a nuclear strike, immune.

Laser testing by the Soviets continues on the ground, another possible basing area for a laser satellite weapon, and one that would save the Soviets the expense of lifting heavy equipment off the earth. In March 1983, when a U.S. satellite mysteriously disappeared over Soviet territory, many intelligence officials believed the Soviets had conducted their first crude effort to destroy space installations using ground-based lasers. There is a great deal of controversy in the intelligence community about that satellite. But the controversy underlines one of the beauties of a laser attack on U.S. satellites: It is virtually invisible, near impossible to prove.

Meanwhile, the Soviets continue to increase the efficiency of their existing weapons. In 1982, they refined their ability to prepare and launch anti-satellite rockets within 90 minutes. Speed might prove critical in any of the scenarios envisioned for use of the Soviet anti-satellite techniques.

One such scenario might be an outbreak of conventional hostilities in Europe, the Middle East, or any other geopolitical hot spot. Few realize the extent to which U.S. and NATO forces already are reliant on satellite communications. Seventy-five percent of all American long-haul military communications are now conducted by satellite. Our satellites monitor the movement of our own and foreign troops, ships, submarines, and artillery. In time of battle they would be used to guide and track our own forces and some of our weapons. New NATO strategies call for even greater use of satellite communications and guidance technologies in the coming years. The U.S. has already launched six of 18 satellites that will form its Global Positioning System, or "Navstar," by 1988. This network will be able to tell U.S. ships, planes, and tanks their location within 30 feet of altitude, longitude and latitude, and to compute their speed within four inches per second. All these capabilities are remarkable, but they are also an Achilles heel if left unprotected.

A frightening example of how the Soviet anti-satellite strategy might be used came during a session of Soviet war gaming on June 18, 1982. As described by U.S. and European intelligence analysis, the game ran as follows:

> 1. The morning of June 18, an anti-satellite ground weapon was fired from its ground launcher in the Soviet Union. It was aimed at a craft, Cosmos 1375, that had been shot up in preparation two weeks earlier. Cosmos was a near-orbit satellite similar in flight to some U.S. early warning satellites. At 2:30 P.M. Moscow time, Cosmos 1375 was knocked out as it passed over Europe.

2. Following the successful Soviet intercept, Soviet generals fired a wave of Soviet nuclear missiles at mock targets in the Kernechartka region of the Soviet Union. The pattern of the firing, and the different types of missiles used, seemed to indicate they were to simulate simultaneous launches at the United States and Western Europe.

3. From the White Sea, a Soviet Delta class submarine launched a ballistic missile, one of the Russians' most accurate submarine weapons. In real war, it might have been directed at an American population center or, because it is so accurate, a U.S. bomber base. (Submarines with sufficiently accurate missiles are the logical modus operandi for an attack on U.S. bombers. The subs can float near U.S. bases on ostensibly routine missions and deliver a quick hit on the second leg of America's triad.)

4. To complete the exercise, the Soviets fired a pair of missiles which, after leaving the Earth's atmosphere, turned around and headed back toward the Soviet Union. This boomerang firing permitted the Russians to test sophisticated new ballistic missile defense systems. These systems would be expected to come under attack if the United States decided to retaliate for a Soviet first strike.

With some effort, you can view these activities as just another nuclear test. We conduct them, the Europeans conduct them, the Soviets conduct them. Nonetheless, the degree of integration and planning for the tests suggests that this was not simply another test. Standard nuclear tests involve a simple function check on a single weapons system: Does it fire? Is it accurate? Does it blow up? And standard nuclear war-gaming involves *theoretical* scenarizing from data obtained from those function tests. In recent years, the Soviets have departed from these limited, standard tests. They have escalated them, if you will, into complete war-flight games carried out not on blackboards but with real weapons. *Aviation Week and Space Technology,* a journal noted for its accuracy and restraint, wrote of the test: "The U.S.S.R. had conducted a number of simulation tests in the past but has failed (until now) to integrate the high level of command, control, and communications required to conduct a nuclear weapons attack, the ability to destroy U.S. spacecraft in low orbit, and ballistic missile defense against U.S. retaliatory responses."

American apologists for the tests say the Soviets are merely conducting *second strike* exercises, and, hence, the tests ought to be regarded as defensive in nature. (One wonders what the reaction to these tests would be of they had been conducted not by the Kremlin, but by the White House.) That reading contradicts two important data.

Datum one: The Soviets were testing their ability to knock out U.S. early warning satellites. The only function of those satellites is to warn the United States that it is under nuclear attack. They cannot, say, fire weapons at the Soviet Union. It follows that there is no advantage to wiping out those satellites, in effect blinding us from a coming punch, unless such a punch is to be delivered or threatened.

Datum two: The Soviet test was not based on defensive assumptions—that is, that the U.S. had struck first. Such a defensive test would emphasize reaction and response on the part of military and civilian officians. Because the effects of a U.S. first strike would not be predictable, you would want to shove your generals in a room and see how they reacted to chaos—to situations in which, for example, the U.S. first strike had obliterated all Soviet missiles west of the Urals, or destroyed half the Russian submarine fleet, or cut off communications between Yuri Andropov and the army. Only an attacker can fully plan and coordinate; the retaliator must respond. The Soviet test was based on attack assumptions; conditions were non-stressful, systems were working, communications were perfect.

The point, of course, is not to send the reader scurrying to the bomb shelters. Whether the Soviet Union decides to take the next logical step—to move from all-out test to all-out conflict—this World War III dry run points to the importance space defense already plays in strategic calculations. In that sense, it is not a question whether "Star Wars" systems can be operable by 1985 or the 21st century, or whether Star Wars can be avoided altogether by treaties and promises and assurances. Star Wars is here; space, as John F. Kennedy put it, "is a sea, and a sea on which we must sail."

Another possible use for anti-satellite weaponry carries grave implications for arms control. With a fully operational capability against U.S. satellites, the Soviets might decide to assert that U.S. satellite overflights are a violation of Russian air space. International agreements have always left open the question of where air space stops and outer space begins; there is a tacit, but not explicit understanding by most nations that any installation in orbit is free to float where it likes. Should the Soviets wish to challenge that understanding, they would only have to say so. Other countries, lacking any capability comparable to the Soviet satellite warfare weapons, could object but do little. The consequences would be great. Such a declaration would call into question most of the intelligence satellites, for example, that the United States uses to monitor Soviet arms production—in particular, to determine if the Kremlin is complying, or not complying with arms control agreements. It would be ironic, indeed, if the U.S., by restraining itself from competition for the use of space, undercut its ability to limit the far deadlier weapons of mass destruction now on the ground. Perhaps more frightening is the fact that the Kremlin might decide to extend its satellite quarantine to friendly countries in the Middle East and Europe, which would cut off our vital conventional reconnaissance satellites from these regions as well. And the United States would have almost no options. As Dr. Jastrow writes: "If the Soviet Union demanded that foreign satellites stay out of the space above its territory, there would be little that the United States could do. As of this moment, Moscow has killer satellites; Washington has none. We would only be able to respond to restrictions on our freedom to move around in space through military actions on the ground, something an American president might find difficult to initiate."

Satellite warfare, of course, is just one tactical objective in a rather broad Soviet strategy to exploit the military and economic potential of space. Another long-standing goal is to establish a permanent manned space presence. The Soviets took a big step toward that goal when a crew of cosmonauts occupied the Salyut 6 space station for 185 days in 1980. They took another in 1981 when Salyut 6 hooked up in orbit with Cosmos 1267. One Soviet official called it a "building block approach" that would allow the Soviets to construct a large station for further testing, maintenance, surveillance, and, of course, Soviet power projection in space. A manned platform would be an ideal basing ground for Soviet laser weaponry, if, indeed, it is being contemplated. It would give the Soviets an advantage in developing and refining space-age industrial techniques. It might also, according to a Pentagon spokesman, serve as "the forerunner of a weapons platform." Whatever uses the Soviets intend for such a manned space station or stations, such uses are broad, and a manned presence in space would give the Kremlin a leg up in the ultimate military and economic frontier.

It should be noted that the stationing of weapons of mass destruction in outer space is already prohibited by the Outer Space Treaty of 1967. The Soviets and the U.S. both pledge continued fealty to this agreement. Hence, most U.S. plans for space have centered around the idea of "clean wars," in which weapons would be aimed basically at other weapons— really rather a benign concept compared to the prospect of mutual assured destruction on earth. The mere fact that weapons may not come from space, however, does not mean that the consequences of strategic inferiority in this theatre would be less than tragic. Moscow's World War III test is just one example of how serious inferiority could be. Further-more, a treaty banning mass murder systems in space is no guarantee they will not be stationed there, as Helsinki, SALT I and II, the ABM treaty, and the chemical weapons ban bitterly prove. So do a whole series of unilateral U.S. gestures to promote peace in space. In the 1960s, for instance, the United States actually had an anti-satellite system involving ground-launched missiles. The system was dismantled in 1975 in hopes that the Soviets would follow suit and avoid development of their own anti-satellite system. They did not.

Probably the most frightening aspect of the Soviet space effort, and one of the most heavily funded branches, is the division that has concentrated on the design of just such weapons-from-space hardware. Since the mid-1960s, the Soviets have conducted more than 20 tests on systems to deliver nuclear warheads at the United States and Europe using satellites. One such system, the Fractional Orbit Bombardment System, involves the launch of nuclear warheads over the South Pole. The October 18, 1982, *New York Times* reported on a similar "orbital bombing system that could rain warheads on the United States from space. . . . But try as they may, American military planners can find no value in space bombs when thousands of nuclear missiles are already poised for Armageddon here on earth." If American military planners have tried as they may and found no use for such weaponry, they are not very good tryers. Firing weapons over the South Pole, for example, would enable the Soviets to launch a nuclear strike that would occur completely undetected by our early warning satellites, which rest, Maginot-line-like, above the North. Even if the U.S. stationed warning satellites in the South, weapons delivery systems like the Fractional Orbit system would give the Soviets a tremendous strategic advantage. Even weapons traveling in only a partial orbit would be more ambiguous in character than an intercontinental missile; it would take the United States hours or days longer to determine if a group of firings represented a joint satellite launch, a cluster of anti-satellite weapons, or a full-fledged nuclear attack. Other weapons, moreover, might travel several orbits, or several hundred. In that way, hundreds of nuclear warheads would be poised, ready to rain down on the United States with little or no warning.

In their 1965 book, *Strike From Space,* Chester Ward and Phyllis Schlafly presaged Soviet steps to achieve just such a capability. They were laughed out of the ideological ballpark as intergalactic chicken littles. Today, whether or not the Soviets proceed very far with such a capability, there is no serious doubt that they have refined it. *Strike From Space* erred only in being a little too farsighted, and, perhaps, in failing to see that the Soviets would seek to achieve a strike-from-space capability even after signing the 1967 agreement proscribing such weapons.

American efforts in space have been hampered, more than anything else, by our government's hesitation to proclaim that, yes, America seeks a leading role there. Military and civilian programs for space have been rigorously kept separate, at the insistence not just of the Congress or of disarmament advocates, but the military itself. The Soviet approach to space has been just the opposite. It stresses integration of programs. It recognizes that much technology will have both military and economic applications, and instead of worrying about which technology belongs where, sets about developing the technology that will advance both programs. This laudable sense of purpose is lacking in U.S. programs.

In an interview with science editor George Alexander of *The Los Angeles Times,* space scientist Joseph Bruman of the Jet Propulsion Laboratory near Pasadena, California, describes the difference: "The Russians don't think in terms of specific goals like we do. We set ourselves a target and a date—go to the moon by the end of the decade or land on Mars by 1976—and then try to make good on it. The Soviets, on the other hand, are committed to developing a broad spectrum of capabilities. When an opportunity presents itself . . . the Soviets try to capitalize on it. They play a patient game, building a series of blocks. If they can keep a crew alive, that's a block. If they develop a shielding to protect people from interplanetary space, that's a block. If they develop a new generation of big boosters, that's a block."

Instead of enforcing a somewhat artificial distinction between military research and civilian research, the Soviet program aims to develop important core technologies of space which, in turn, will have applications in both fields: increasing Soviet launch capability, placing men in space, reducing the size and weight of circuits and other components, improving communications, and so on. In some areas, the United States has been able to score stunning successes despite its haphazard approach. Overall, though, the Soviet Union, despite its enormous handicaps in any kind of technological competition, is again back in the race.

A missile defense in space would, in and of itself, correct many U.S. vulnerabilities. It would be in a position to protect not just our cities, which are certainly the top priority, but also to thwart any attack on our vital installations in space. Furthermore, the high priority, Manhattan Project approach recommended for building such a space defense would fit in nicely with the broader need to reemphasize space as a potential theatre of action, and with the requirement that we move quickly to reduce the vulnerability of our intelligence and command satellites. Defense, in other words, is the answer to more than the strategic imbalance on the ground. It would be a logical and quick corrective to the growing imbalance outlined above.

The United States has begun to take note of Soviet progress in space; in many ways, improving our effort to match that program would involve simple acceleration. (Simple, but significant acceleration, given that the Soviet spending on space, as a share of Soviet production, is five times that of the U.S.) A good example of both the achievements and failures of U.S. efforts is our response to the Soviet anti-satellite threat.

Protecting a satellite from anti-satellite weapons can be achieved in any of several ways, all of which are now actively under study by the Pentagon. Satellites can be made mobile, equipped with small rocket motors enabling them to evade attacking missiles or satellite mines. Lt. General Richard C. Henry, deputy commander of the newly organized Space Command in the Air Force, says evasion technologies offer the greatest promise of protection for our satellites. Satellites can also be disguised. Scientists report that the same technology used to build the U.S. Stealth bomber—which escapes the eye of radar by using special paints and other deflectors—can be applied to satellites. American satellites now being designed are constructed with these features in mind.

Another important means of protection is hardening. Sensitive electronic equipment now deployed in space can easily be knocked out by setting off a single, large explosion to create an electromagnetic pulse—or, by aiming a similar series of pulses at individual U.S. satellites. Hardening also diminishes the damage that might result from impact with shrapnel or debris.

In addition, there are a whole range of countermeasures to an attack on our satellites, of which active defense measures from an anti-missile defense is just one. One of the earliest uses of ground-based lasers might be to shoot down projectiles aimed at our satellites: an anti-anti-satellite weapon.

There is, finally, the possibility of developing American

anti-satellite weapons to shoot down Soviet targets. America unilaterally withdrew from this competition in the mid-1970s, as we have said, but there is no reason to stay out of it as long as the Soviet Union fails to reciprocate. Contracts worth $770 million have been awarded to adapt the F-15 fighter plane for anti-satellite purposes, and research continues on laser anti-satellite weapons and projectiles similar to the Soviet attack vehicles.

Indeed, one of the regrettable aspects of the U.S. program to protect its satellites is its emphasis on attacking Soviet satellites—an ironic recapitulation, perhaps, of MAD nuclear strategy. The threat to destroy Soviet satellites is certainly one worth having. Far more important, however, are those programs which would protect our own satellites. If the Soviets, for example, should decide to attack our satellites in conjunction with a nuclear first strike, a later threat by us to destroy their satellites, after they have already wiped out our cities or major military installations or both, would be of little use. And, given the more heavy reliance of U.S. and NATO forces on high-technology satellite communications, the mutual capability to destroy one another's satellites hardly amounts to a balance: The Soviets can do without their satellites in the event of conventional war in Europe. We cannot.

The question is not whether U.S. officials recognize that there is a threat and are doing something about it. The problem is whether America is moving too slowly. "No matter what the United States does to catch up now, the next few years are almost certain to be a time of Soviet domination in space," Dr. Jastrow writes. "It remains to be seen whether the magnitude of the current effort will be sufficient to meet the challenge." In a November 1982 press conference, Secretary of Defense Caspar Weinberger confirmed that the Reagan administration seeks a far greater emphasis on defense from space. He went on to say, though, that work on such defenses was probably "15 years down the road." It probably is, given the attitude of many public officials—even those within the space program. Just a month earlier, Reagan science adviser George Keyworth warned *against* any dramatic American moves into space: "Headlong rushes to develop a system," he said, "will ultimately compromise our prospects for the future." If, indeed, a serious American space program is 15 years off, under current arrangements, that is all the more argument to change those arrangements. The Soviets are not waiting for Buck Rogers and Artoo Deetoo. They are moving into space now.

A serious effort to match the Soviets in space must aim for several objectives. Priority one would be to reduce the cost of transporting items into space. This, as we have noted, would fit in neatly with construction of an anti-missile defense in space. Today's space shuttle is a start, and is proving to be more efficient than any previous system. The shuttle, though, was designed more with short term development costs than long term economics in mind. Available hardware, such as strap-on boosters, was used to minimize the up-front shuttle budget and, thus, enhance its chances for approval. Hence, even as the shuttle was built, it was not the most efficient system available.

Today, scientists say space transport costs could be cut to 10 percent or less of current shuttle rates within five years. NASA scientists Ian Bekey and John E. Naugle published an assessment of the potential for transport cost reductions, *Just Over the Horizon in Space, Astronautics, and Aeronautics*, in May 1980. They see substantial potential savings: "The shuttle will not do better than $1,000 to transport one kilogram into orbit, compared to only $5 to fly one kilogram in an airliner from Los Angeles to New York [even though] the energy requirements are the same. The costs of the equivalent electrical energy comes to only about 50 cents, leaving a lot of room for improvement." Bekey and Naugle expect better systems—operating like an air cargo airline—to reduce the costs of space transportation "by at least two orders of magnitude." The Boeing Company has already submitted a formal proposal to the U.S. Air Force for production of a spacecraft, the Air Launched Sortie Vehicle, that would leave the ground atop a modified 747 jetliner, and then rocket out into space on its own. Such a craft could take off, land at any large airport, would be available for quick missions, and would reduce the shuttle's cost-per-kilo costs by at least 50 percent. The technology is not lacking; a coherent U.S. space program, seeking to develop core technologies that will provide both military and civilian benefits, is. Other core goals—obtaining economies of scale through mass production of certain space systems, establishing a manned presence in space to test for commercial applications—are well within reach, but will not be met without a commitment by the United States to move into this high frontier of space.

Our concern here is largely for military strategy and capabilities. We must not overlook, however, the important economic benefits of space—and the contribution a strong economy makes to a strong defense. A number of military reformers have reminded us of this contribution in recent years; they are not to be ignored. Industrial capacity, energy supplies, access to raw materials, even the general morale and health of the people—these and other factors are often the real difference in an evenly distributed balance of power. Military men throughout history have stressed the strategic importance of seemingly non-strategic factors. In his great treatise on naval might, *The Influence of Sea Power on History*, Admiral Alfred Thayer Mahan outlines "the principal conditions affecting the sea power of nations: I. Geographical Position. II. Physical Conformation, including, as connected therewith, natural productions and climate. III. Extent of Territory. IV. Number of Population. V. Character of the People. VI. Character of the Government, including, therein, the national institutions." Mahan's history of sea power from 1660 to 1783 concludes that it was the British merchant fleet, more than the British Navy itself, that guaranteed His Majesty's government superiority on the high seas. Just so, the country that makes the most serious commitment to the peaceful, economic exploitation of space will probably find itself in the best military position as well. It will also help provide an expanding economy for its own people and its trading partners that will pay back investments in space many times over.

The benefits of our early efforts in space are all around us. Nearly 30,000 transatlantic telephone circuits are already in use. Operating through about 120 orbiting satellites, the world's new communications network carries millions of phone calls, television broadcasts, and other messages every day. The human side of all this communications hardware was brought home late in 1982 when a Soviet satellite spotted a group of Canadian and American sailors floating at sea. They were fished out of the ocean a few hours later.

Satellite communications alone are expected to do $10 billion a year in business before 1990. American observation satellites track and estimate air pollution; help locate oil, natural gas, and scarce minerals; direct fishermen to the best spots on the world's oceans; enhance weather forecasting and predict damage to crops; and provide a broad range of other important services. Dozens of indirect benefits have accrued to our economy as techniques and products developed for the space industry are applied to commerce on the ground. Plastics, metals, and crystals introduced through space research are now used in surgery and biological studies. The development of microchips and miniature transitors, spurred on by NASA's need for smaller electronic components, has spawned vast new industries.

The opportunities will be even broader in the coming years. Private companies are already exploring the idea of their own launchings into space. A group of Texas investors launched a small rocket in September 1982 in preparation for development of a "low-cost, market-oriented" shuttle business. A company in Princeton, New Jersey, offered NASA $1 billion late in 1982 to purchase one of its space shuttles, a deal that would leave NASA in charge of operations but grant the firm the right to market its services. The unique environment of space—zero gravity, an almost perfect vacuum, sterile conditions, and almost unlimited heat absorbtion—promises a number of new industries and production techniques as the shuttle and systems like it bring down transportation costs.

Farther down the road, but perhaps not much farther, space offers a source of virtually limitless energy: the sun. Solar collection panels placed in orbit would collect the sun's energy almost directly, without the filtering effect of dust, clouds, and molecules in the earth's atmosphere. This power can be beamed down to earth through microwave transmissions. Large collection grids on the earth, and huge antennae in orbit, will be needed to make such solar generators efficient, but size in and of itself is not necessarily a great barrier. The Department of Energy conducted studies on the subject from 1977 and 1981 and found no immediate technological barriers. The Department estimated that a solar generating station in space might produce 1.6 trillion kilowatt hours of power over 40 years. Even if such a system cost $12.5 billion, it would generate electricity at an average cost of five cents per kilowatt hour, a figure that makes it already competitive with coal and nuclear power plants now in operation.

To achieve these and even more ambitious goals in space, America need only repeat what it did on its last frontier, the West. We would have to provide for reasonable means of transportation—a railroad into space. We would have to create human outposts to coordinate and oversee our increasing activity—a town store or post office above the atmosphere. We would have to proclaim, and then demonstrate, our determination to defend the frontier settler and his possessions—a sheriff's office in the sky. We should be doing this and more anyway, in order to protect the United States and its allies on earth. We would do well to take advantage of this frontier with the same cunning and courage our ancestors applied to theirs.

VI

Defense and
Military Reform

GENERAL ROBERT C. RICHARDSON, formerly a top procurement and planning officer for the U.S. Air Force, has a favorite old proverb: "For want of a nail, the shoe was lost; for want of the shoe, the horse was lost; for want of the horse, the battle was lost." It is an adage that underlines what many are coming to regard as the central source of American weakness, which is not a too-small Pentagon budget (though larger budgets are needed), nor the all-volunteer services, which have begun at last to click on recruitment. Simply, the problem with the American military is this: It has become as wasteful, inefficient, and bureaucratic as the rest of the government and the society.

How America buys weapons is not a glamorous subject. For decades most of the military debate has focused around nothing more sophisticated than dollars and cents totals. When it goes beyond, as it has in recent years, it is generally to consider grand, new strategies: shifting our emphasis from land forces to the navy, moving to higher (or simpler) technology, and bolder (or less bold) tactics on the ground, or, for our purposes here, building a true defense against nuclear weapons. How we carry out these schemes is perceived as hopelessly tedious, technical matters best left within the bowels of the Pentagon.

To address American strength and strategy meaningfully,

however, we had best consider the question of how we build our strength. How we decide what weapons to build, and how we build them, can make the difference between a weapon taking five years to construct and costing, say, $1 billion, or, as many weapons do now, taking fifteen years, costing $5 billion, and ending up so over-designed and discussed that it is a less effective weapon than it was to begin with.

There are political imperatives as well. Only a military rebuilding program that proceeds efficiently can sustain public backing. As the Heritage Foundation's George Kuhn, a former Army officer, writes in *Agenda '83:* "Americans rightly expect decisive improvements in defense capability. A military program that demonstrates tangible progress toward these improvements will be given public support even in the face of pressure to reduce spending. One that gains public support and then fails to translate its added resources into added strength will certainly lose that support."

In recent years, a loosely formed group, vaguely referred to as the "military reformers," that includes Senator Gary Hart (D. Colo.), Pentagon systems analyst Franklin Spinney and other "mavericks," scholar Kuhn and other think-tankers, has focused some useful attention on the problem of how to make the Pentagon lean but mean once again. Some of their suggestions would save billions of dollars annually. One oft-proposed reform would be to open up the procurement process to more competitive bidding, a change that would reduce the cost of many weapons by as much as 20 percent.

Another reform would simply reduce the number of regulations and the amount of paperwork involved with routine Pentagon operations. The Carter administration began a thorough review of needless regulation that was continued and expanded by the Reagan administration. These and other suggestions would either save billions or, for the same billions, buy more weapons.

What the military reform movement has not done is to develop a comprehensive understanding of why the Pentagon has grown more and more inefficient since the Vietnam era. There is a broad consensus, among politicians, the public, and even military officers, about the problems: the production of boondoggle, gold-plated weapons; the stretching-out of manufacturing schedules and the stretching-up of budgets; and the congressional horse-trading system that reduces decisions important to national security to such geographical analyses of which jet fighter component is manufactured in Tip O'Neill's congressional district. But the reform movement has yet to identify the central cause of all these problems: considerations of time.

If an American president decided right now, as he is reading this, that the country needs a major change in military strategy, the country's military leaders would tell him that the hardware to carry out that strategy would take 15 to 30 years to build. It takes that long for Congress and one or more administrations to debate and decide to research a proposed weapon; to ante up money for development and design; to re-debate and alter (usually several times) the design to their specifications of acceptability; to order, produce, and test early prototype models of the weapon; to analyze, quantify, and re-debate the test results; to decide whether to buy the weapon, or not to buy it, or to put off a decision on buying it; to appropriate the money for production, enduring a host of criticism of the new weapon from domestic critics and allies, and a multitude of comparisons with this-or-that simpler or better or cheaper weapon; and, through several years of actual procurement and deployment, the most expensive stage of the process and, thus, the most attractive place to cut, to stick with it.

It takes better than 15 years to move through that acquisition cycle with its delaying and cost-multiplying pitfalls. The MX missile, first proposed in the early 1970s as the logical followup to our aging Minuteman force, will not be fully deployed until 1989—if, in fact, it is approved, and then built without any further delays. Other controversial weapons systems of recent memory have traveled the same long and winding road. The Stealth radar-evading bomber. The B-1 bomber. The 600-ship navy. The Cruise missile. Not one took less than a dozen years to move from idea to drawing board to battlefield.

The 15-year acquisition process, as Gen. Richardson likes

to put it, is "the tail that wags the dog" for military strategists, congressional committees, and presidents. Any new system, any new strategy, must realistically be evaluated in terms of long lead times, cost overruns, and red tape. No wonder an air of stagnation has crept into the Pentagon budget debate in recent years. Instead of deciding what strategies and weapons are important, and tailoring acquisition methods and bureaucracies to meet them, the fact of bureaucracy and delays is allowed to dictate what can be done. The result was nicely captured in the *New York Post*'s lead editorial of February 15, 1983:

> Representative Joseph Addabbo, chairman of the House Defense Appropriations subcommittee, wants to scrap the B-1 bomber, the F-18 fighter-bomber, and two nuclear-powered carriers. The Congressional Budget Office, which is supposed to specialize in accounting, not military strategy, proposes cancelling the MX missile, the F-18, and 63 Navy destroyers. Representative Les Aspin of the House Armed Services Committee plans to hold yet more hearings. Representative Ronald Dellums wants to "expose my colleagues to a different perspective."
>
> How many perspectives can Congress get?
>
> According to the *Armed Forces Journal,* Congress held an incredible 407 separate hearings last year [1982] between Feb. 8 and Sept. 30—when, by law, it should have but had not passed the 1983 defense budget.
>
> During that period, 1,258 hapless Pentagon officials spent hundreds of hours testifying before Congressional committees. The printed record fills up four feet of shelf space—and still doesn't cover the last three months of the year.
>
> There are six separate Congressional committees obsessed with defense. How ridiculous. After one hearing, a Pentagon official was sent 150 pages of typewritten follow-up questions to answer for the record.
>
> If Defense Secretary Weinberger and his colleagues were allowed more time to manage the defense of the United States, they might find the time to consider whether all those weapons now on order are really necessary.

All that bureaucracy—much of it, ironically, designed to keep military costs in line—not only imposes a crushing burden on attempts to rebuild American strength in general, it imposes a particular burden on strategists who prefer to re-build it in a new way. Think tanks, committees, and Pentagon programmers develop a vested interest in the way things are, and military interest groups are as entrenched as any lobbyist around. As Pentagon critic William Lind, an aide to Gary Hart, notes:

> Virtually all components of our armed services are large bureaucracies, and the process of selecting a new weapon, or planning a mission, is one of brokering and log-rolling: "If my shop lets yours get that assignment or mission, then mine gets this other one in return." The focus in such a brokering proc-ess is not external—on the enemy—but internal—on how to come up with something everyone in the bureaucracy can live with. This internal political process is stressful, intricate, and time-consuming. Changing a decision means going back into the tank, back into the endless meetings, the hair-pulling and -splitting, the threats to careers if some interests don't get their share. No one wants to alter a compromise once arrived at . . .

MAD strategy—a classic amalgam of interests in the Pentagon, the State Department, and Congress, an unlikely and tenuous alliance of arms controllers and arms builders—draws on this general institutional inertia, as does any existing strategy. Defense systems face the 15-30-year pro-curement cycle that has undermined every major strategic system since the 1960s. The effects of military bureaucratiza-tion are so deleterious that they merit a bit of discussion on their own demerits.

The first major cost imposed by time is: cost. In an inter-view with *Time* magazine in February 1982, a major arms producer, Paul Thayer, Chairman of LTV Corporation, put the tab at 40 cents on the dollar: "Forty cents out of every dollar we charge for every airplane delivered to the govern-ment is attributable to bureaucratic redtape, paperwork, and duplication." Delay a system a year and you add another year's inflation. Set up a new committee asking new ques-tions, and add another staff member to handle the busy work. Perform another review and add redesigns; new fea-tures, old arguments. It all takes time, and time costs money. A study conducted by the General Accounting Office concludes that, on the average, every year added to the acquisition cycle adds 30 percent to the cost of building a weapon.

And the cost goes well beyond dollars. Another heavy tab is the price inflexibility. By the time the country has even decided to proceed with the development and testing of a weapon, six years have elapsed. At that point, the United States already has a heavy investment in a system, so even if it is beginning to look like a loser, the tendency is to find new functions for a weapon that can't perform its original mission, or add new features to upgrade its performance. Generally, it means more testing and study. Given the choice between saying "yes," "no," or "maybe," most Pentagon planners and politicians prefer to say maybe—thus spreading the responsibility for decisions to past and future decision-makers or, even more fundamentally, avoiding the need to decide at all.

What it all means is that an American president is virtually hamstrung when it comes to dealing with new threats and new opportunities. Any new strategy may not even begin until another president is in office. Conversely, any president must accept virtually every strategic assumption made by his predecessors. The weapons we build today are weapons conceived during the end of Lyndon Johnson's administration and the beginning of Richard Nixon's—before the end of the Vietnam war, before the MIRVing of missiles, and a decade before such important conflicts as the Falklands battle and the Israeli occupation of southern Lebanon. To put it another way, imagine if the Apollo program, launched by John F. Kennedy in 1963, had been run through the military industrial complex of 1983. On a fifteen-year cycle, our first man would have landed on the moon not in 1969, but 1978. On a twenty-year cycle, we would just now be preparing for the lunar landing. But even that is only assuming that Congress, over 20 years of space debate, would not by now have scrapped the program altogether.

The inertia imposed by these and similar pressures frustrates any proposal for innovation. Our commander in chief pilots a great ship, incapable of turning the rudder more than 2 degrees.

A related problem, a third cost of acquisition time snags, is indecision. Anyone familiar with the defense debate knows the "better-system-coming" problem. As time rambles on, systems that did involve the cutting edge of technology lose their advantage. A weapon ready to be built now is up against a better weapon just a few years down the road. We can either build obsolete weapon A now, in greater numbers, or kill it, wait for weapon B, and go through the same debate when weapon B is ready but weapon C looks even better. Indecision, inertia, delays, redesign—all these phenomena feed off one another in a vicious synergism.

Even if America could afford all the costs of this unwieldy acquisition process and somehow manage to field up-to-date weapons in reasonable numbers, the procurement knot would still pose deadly problems for the United States. For while we dally, the Soviets move. The Kremlin's extensive and well-documented intelligence network is busy collecting information and technology on American systems, not from the day they are deployed, or the day they are built, or the day they are designed, but within a year or two that the idea for a new weapon is even proposed. Within a few years, the Soviets assembled the basic building blocks of our technology and are busy (1) working on ways to defeat it and (2) figuring out ways to build it before we do. The Soviet Backfire bomber began as a response to America's B-1 program; it was actually deployed beforehand. The Soviets may also deploy a Stealth-technology plane before the United States. And they might deploy the first effective defense against nuclear missiles years before the United States is even finished studying proposed revisions in the ABM treaty.

The procurement knot, in other words, may guarantee American inferiority in weapons. It would be ironic if a society that cannot feed its own people should defeat the United States in a race for ideas and strategies and high technology. Yet that is precisely what is happening. There are only two means, by and large, of competing with the Soviet Union for superior arms. We can build similar systems in equal numbers, hoping against hope to out-produce an economy that is small and weak, but that has the option to extort work from Gulag laborers and, indeed, the general population. Or, we can build better weapons. Building better weapons requires flexibility, action, and a cutting-edge philosophy that enables us to perform regular end runs around the unwieldy Soviet bureaucracy. But this second course—really, our only hope of competing—cannot be followed if our Pentagon is more cumbersome than even the Kremlin.

It wasn't always like this, and the way it once was is a good model for those who want to improve the way it is now. In 1950, it took the political system twelve months to evaluate a proposal, research and develop individual technologies, and decide whether or not to proceed. That process, the "front-end decision" by Congress and the president, today takes an average of six years or more. The time needed to draw up and produce the B-47 bomber took eighteen months in 1947. As late as the 1950s, it took only five to six years for such bold technological initiatives as the Atlas, Apollo, and Polaris programs. Today—in the case of the B-1 and Stealth bombers—production takes twelve years and then some.

Remember: As a rule of thumb, every year added to the production cycle of a new weapon adds roughly 30 percent to the final cost of producing the weapon. Add another year, and you are adding another year's inflation in labor and raw materials costs. Delay or scale down production, and you are adding to the costs and uncertainties of the company making the weapon; it raises its prices accordingly. Add in another year's design changes, and you are raising costs still further.

It is small wonder, given the increasing involvement of politicians and their staffs in the very engineering of a weapon, that weapons regularly take three times as long, and cost five to ten times as much, as originally projected. During the Roosevelt, Truman, Eisenhower, and Kennedy years, weapons regularly came in ahead of schedule and under budget. During those years, however, decisions were made by a few readily identifiable program chiefs in the Pentagon, and their decisions were carried out, for better or worse, in a few years. By contrast, late in 1982, the manufacturer of the Stealth bomber met with Air Force officials to inform them that the plane could be produced as much as two years ahead of schedule. The manufacturer was turned down: The military decided that speeding up Stealth might threaten a bird in the hand—the B-1 bomber—scheduled to move into production sooner.

As Richardson wrote in the *Washington Report,* a publication of the American Security Council, in November 1982: "The U.S. built pioneering, high-technology systems such as our first ICBM (Atlas), our first nuclear powered submarine, and our first manned satellite [Mercury] in five to six years from a standing start. We flew the first prototype of a high-technology bomber, the B-47, 18 months after the start of the program. Why can't we do the same for the new systems . . . in the 1980s?"

Attempts to untie that knot have had, in many cases, the unfortunate effect of making it still tighter. Military reformers would be the first to admit, indeed, to caution, that as a group they present no coherent program for change. They share an apprehension, but not a strategy. To the extent that a common strain exists in most reform analysis, though, it is that "high-technology boondoggles" generate expensive "gold-plated" weapons systems, and that, moreover, simpler weapons that work should be built instead of overly-complex super-weapons.

In some cases, these observations have led to worthwhile suggestions. Military reformers generally want to open up the production process to more competition, a change that might save 10 to 20 percent in costs per system. They want to impose the burden of cost overruns on weapons contractors instead of the taxpayer, a good idea, but one, of course, that cannot be applied fairly in cases where congressional committees ask the contractor to redesign the weapon they bid on. But all the savings to be garnered by these and other organizational reforms are peanuts placed against that inexorable 30-percent-a-year time factor. They do nothing to address the five-and-a-half years of political uncertainty added to the front end decision process.

There is a sense, however, in which the military reformers are efficiency's worst enemy. In their efforts to stamp out every possible boondoggle, every stray bit of high technology, the reformers generally advocate more testing, more analysis, more review. These are the very "reforms" initiated under Robert McNamara in the 1960s that undercut the

Pentagon's efficiency to begin with. There will always be the opportunity, if no restraints are imposed, for more debate and more equivocating, no matter how much a weapon is tested. What is needed to make the military truly efficient is a dose of leadership from American politicians—a willingness, on the one hand, to make a tough decision and stick with it, and, on the other hand, to get Congress out of the business of engineering weapons, and to leave the nuts and bolts affairs of the military up to the experts.

Because the reform movement has failed to grasp the central cause—time—it sees only a profusion of effects, and often suggests ideas that would stretch acquisition time still further. The reformers, in a military sense, are good scouts, identifying all the enemy forces and movements on the procurement battlefield. But they have been poor generals. A revealing example came to light in a *Time* magazine cover story published March 7, 1983. The article cited as a "classic case" of waste and confusion the Viper antitank weapon designed in 1971.

> Ten years ago, the Army decided to provide infantrymen with cheap, light antitank bazookas. The Vipers were projected to cost about $75 apiece. But design changes began almost as soon as the weapon was proposed. The weight, it was decided, must be reduced to no less than seven pounds. This meant the warhead had to weigh less than a pound, which sharply limited its potential destructive power. The size of the rocket motor was also reduced to cut blast noise. By the time the contractor finished redesigning it, the Vipers cost not $75, but $787 apiece.

The military reformer's question is, "Why not ten of the original Vipers instead of one of the hi-tech ones?" The military reform reformer's answer is, "Because instead of deciding on the weapon and building it then, we went through a decade of committee revisions."

In the same article, *Time* complains, along with weapons analyst Franklin Spinney, about the failure of Pentagon projections to accurately predict Pentagon costs. Spinney's "two-hour presentation of case studies," *Time* writes, "meticulously demonstrated that a basic cost assumption made by the Pentagon—that the price of each new weapon will significantly decrease as soon as it is being produced at an efficient rate—is fundamentally flawed. 'When we predict long-term price declines, we assume design stability,' he said. In reality, the cost of high-tech systems invariably skyrockets because of unrealistic initial estimates, obsessive design changes, and erratic production rates."

All of that is fine as far as it goes. But it is about as illuminating as saying, "The heat caused the temperature to rise." Why are our weapons plagued by "design instability"? Why must Pentagon planners and manufacturers continue going back to the drawing board to upgrade performance, change missions, re-calculate production estimates? Again, the answer is, because our rapidly obsolescing systems require periodic injections of newer technology to keep them up to date. If we choose not to make the injection, we throw away several years research and development: Why not, instead, try to save the weapon? If we keep adding new features, we marginally improve the weapon, but at the cost of delays and money.

Effective military reform will involve a return to the procedures for deciding on and buying weapons that were used the last time we did that efficiently: in the 1950s. This very solution is suggested by a chart which accompanied the *Time* article. The chart, "less bang for the buck," outlines the decline in purchasing power of the defense dollar. In 1951, 6,300 fighters for $7 billion. In 1981, 322 fighters for $11 billion. In 1953, 6,735 tanks for $2 billion. In 1983, 701 tanks for $2 billion. To anyone reading that chart, the gut reflex is "let's do it the old way."

Doing it the old way will require a reversal of the demilitarization of the Pentagon that occurred in the McNamara era (which also witnessed, not incidentally, the coronation of MAD strategy). Or, to put it another way, it will require us to do things the way we once did them— things that we stopped doing when the McNamara philosophy of "cost-benefit analysis," "low-risk acquisition," "fly-before-you-buy purchasing," and a host of similar dogmas became the rule. Such a reversal will require boldness, flexibility, and strategic innovation.

And with boldness, flexibility, and innovation come risk.

The first military reform that is needed—both on its own merits and, in particular, in order to build a strategic defense—is a reduction of the front end decision process, down from its present six years to the 12–18 months of the 1950s. American politicians are no less capable today than then of reading general weapons reports, weighing strategies and alternative systems for meeting those strategies, and deciding what to build. What will be required is discipline, both from the White House and Congress.

On the one hand, both branches will have to surrender thousands of small, technical decisions to regular military program officers. On the other, both branches will have to provide those officers with *more* strategic direction: clearer missions for the services, for particular weapons, and for particular officers. Handing over the details will remove decisions that ought to be made by experts from the endless haggling of congressional subcommittees. Assigning definite responsibility for particular programs to particular officers will give those officers every incentive to make their program a success. That is exactly what the acquisitions process should do: assign the reward of success—but also the responsibility for failure—to real people. Focusing credit and blame heightens an officer's reason to stick with a weapon he knows will work and to identify a weapon he knows will not.

The second reform springs from the first: Once a decision is made, the decision must stick—at least until a clearly superior weapon can be designed and, through the same streamlined process, approved for several years funding. Once the country decides to go with a weapon, the re-debates and the re-negotiations must, for several years of procurement, cease.

This will require even more political courage than the first reform. Because, under a streamlined procurement process, there will be failures. And when those failures occur, there will be definite, not dispersed, responsibility. Someone will have piloted the weapon from start to finish, particularly as acquisition time is reduced and it again becomes *possible* for the same officer to guide a program from start to finish.

But in the long run, the findable costs of boondoggle weapons, while politically embarrassing, are far less than the dispersed and invisible costs of a 15-year procurement process. As with any other government program, from food stamps to student loans, the temptation for government is to hire more and more bureaucrats, set up more and more committees, and consult more and more think tanks, in an endless and unwinnable battle to eliminate every last ounce of "waste and fraud." In the social programs, this has led to federal and local governments spending an average of $18,000 a year for every poor person in the country—yet finding that less than a third of it reaches the needy. In the Pentagon, it has created a situation where, while there are few bribes, no kickbacks, seldom a system deployed that doesn't work, it is only because we seldom deploy any system at all.

The classic choices offered by military reformers—Should we build three small ships or one big one? Four Sidewinder air-to-air missiles or one Sparrow? One M-1 tank or six M-60s?—is really an evasion of the more fundamental question: Why do they all come in over budget and under performance? America, unless it wants to continue building tanks and missiles and fighter planes using only 1960s technology, cannot forever milk the cheap and attractive weapons that have been rolling off the production lines for years. We will have to build new systems, using new technologies, to fit new strategies. The problem is to make sure that these new systems avoid the overruns and time lags that plague every system we build today. Then we can build Sidewinders *and* Sparrows, carriers *and* destroyers, because someone, somewhere, will have made a real and binding decision.

Reform Three springs from the very limits that any reform program will be able to work on the Department of Defense. The president and Congress must regularly identify high-priority military needs and go outside regular budget procedures, in Congress and the Pentagon, to meet them. Dwight Eisenhower understood the capabilities and shortcomings of the military establishment better than any president in this century. When Eisenhower wanted the country to build an intercontinental missile, therefore, he set up the Von Neumann Commission. Ike didn't ask for "exploratory funding" or "development grants." He gave the commission three months to draw up a prototype missile—or tell him it couldn't be done. The Commission, confounding Ike's experts in the Pentagon, said that it could. The Atlas ICBM was rolling off the production line within four years.

That kind of occasional end run is even more necessary when a president wants to achieve a major new strategy—such as a nuclear strategy that moves from Mutual Assured Destruction to Assured Survival. Once a president makes a firm decision to lead his staff and his country toward a system of defense, as Winston Churchill led Britain toward an anti-bomber defense in the 1930s, most of the technical cavils will vanish. "Technical considerations and political goals act and react upon one another," Churchill recalled in his memoirs (*The Gathering Storm,* New York: Houghton Mifflin Co., 1958). The need for leadership is particularly acute as America confronts the new strategic battleground of space. As William Gregory writes in *Aviation Week and Space Technology* (October 18, 1982): "No strong consensus is evident in industry or government for starting an engineering development program or a space . . . battle station. There is not likely to be one. Decisions on mammoth technical ventures like the development of nuclear weapons or a manned lunar landing are dictated, rather than evolving outgrowths of advances in basic research."

REAGAN'S INITIATIVE: A CASE STUDY

If any proof were needed that strategic defense will not be treated kindly by the Department of Defense, it came with President Reagan's initiative of March 1983. The day after his speech, the President issued an executive order calling for a "thorough study" of the feasibility of building anti-defense missiles. If history is any guide, such a study should have been submitted to a group of independent scientists, former military officers, and industry experts—all well-qualified to evaluate such a proposal, but all independent of the pressures to tailor their findings to produce a predetermined result.

Instead, President Reagan sent his proposal to be studied by the Pentagon. With a blank check to evaluate the feasibility of various proposals, the Defense Department moved on. The institutional pressures on those conducting the study were great. The desired result—a finding that strategic defense has "many advantages" but should be submitted for "further study"—was almost foreordained.

The point is not whether military men hold an irrational or quirky preference for weapons of mass destruction. One of the authors is a military man. Many dedicated people throughout the Pentagon, some in high places, favor a shift to strategic defense. The question, rather, is one of group dynamics. However a program officer or researcher may feel about strategic defense in the abstract, his budget, his career, or his chances for promotion may depend on putting this bold strategy on the back burner. Unless there is a crisis, or a leader at the top ordering his troops to get something done now, the military, like any other bureaucracy, resists change.

It was clear by the summer of 1983 that the Defense Department's evaluation of defense technologies would be anything but detached. At a series of Pentagon briefings in July, private industry officials, anxious to offer technological advances with possible applications to defense, were told not to "emphasize . . . early deployment." The briefing, held by John L. Gardner, Director of Defensive Systems, called on those industry captains to concentrate on "long-term (post the year 2000)" research and development plans. The outline for these briefings is reprinted on the following pages. (See figures 6 and 7.)

The same John L. Gardner, mind you, had already testified before Congress that a strategic missile defense could be built in four to five years at a cost of about $50 billion. (Again, the $50 billion estimate assumed the use of standard acquisition procedures, not a speeded-up program.) Why was he now ruling out the possibility of a near-term resolution in those briefings? If there is, in fact, no way to leap over the hurdles to building a strategic defense except to wait another 20 years, why did the Pentagon bother to tell industry officials this?

The answer was contained in the same briefing. We get it by looking at what the Defense Department *did* want stressed in the strategic defense study. Specifically, the briefing called for programs that "emphasize effectiveness rather than potential for early deployment. . . , [consider] both technology-limited and resource-constrained [elements]. . . , and remain consistent with U.S. obligations under the ABM treaty."

Of course, the only way for the U.S. to remain consistent with its ABM obligations is to either abrogate the agreement or not deploy a space-based ABM. One can argue whether it would be a good idea to renounce this pact or not. But what was this consideration doing in a study of the technical feasibility of strategic defense? Treaties are a matter for presidents and Congress to decide—once the military has provided a broad range of technological facts on which to base their decisions.

The weighing of "resource constraints" mentioned in the briefing outline would appear, also, to be a political matter. Later in the briefing, it was explained that these "constraints" included the protection of current research and development programs, and the assumption that any increase in strategic defense spending would be small. In other words, no one was to propose anything that might threaten other, more favored projects. Whether the nation should radically shift priorities in favor of strategic defense is, of course, open to argument. But again, it is an argument for national leaders to decide—not Pentagon bureaucrats.

The third priority mentioned in the briefing—"effectiveness" over "availability"—has a more appealing ring to it. After all, we don't want to rush headlong into building a system that isn't "effective." This seductive appeal vanishes, however, once we examine how the term "effectiveness" is being used. Whether a system is effective depends on what we expect it to do. If we expect it to knock out 100 percent of any Soviet first strike, we will require one level of effectiveness—a pretty high one. What about 98 percent? Is that "effective"? What if we could build a system that could knock out *half* of a Soviet strike? Would this be of strategic benefit?

One would expect the Pentagon to produce a whole range of different options in such a study. System A will knock out 100 percent of a Soviet attack and will cost $14 trillion. System B will knock out 98 percent and cost $50 billion. System C will take out 30 percent, but only cost $30 billion. Do you

DTST

DTST BRIEFING TO INDUSTRY AND ACADEMIC COMMUNITIES

30 JUNE 1983

0900-1100 MORNING BRIEFING

1330-1530 REPEAT OF MORNING BRIEFING

- BACKGROUND ON DEFENSIVE TECHNOLOGIES STUDY

- CURRENT STATUS

- SCHEDULE FOR REPORTS

- REVIEW OF PANEL QUESTIONS

- FORM FOR OUTSIDE INPUTS

- DISCUSSIONS

JOHN L. GARDNER
DIRECTOR, DEFENSIVE SYSTEMS
OUSDRE

6-28-83-3

| DTST | NSSD 6-83 REQUIREMENTS SUMMARY |

LONG TERM GOAL

- ELIMINATE THE THREAT POSED BY NUCLEAR BALLISTIC MISSILES TO THE SECURITY OF THE U.S. AND ITS ALLIES

REQUIREMENTS

- EVALUATE AND DETERMINE REQUIREMENTS FOR SHIFTING LONG-TERM U.S. STRATEGIC DEFENSE POLICY TOWARD INCREASED RELIANCE ON DEFENSIVE SYSTEMS

- REMAIN CONSISTENT WITH U.S. OBLIGATIONS UNDER THE ABM TREATY

- EMPHASIZE EFFECTIVENESS RATHER THAN POTENTIAL FOR EARLY DEPLOYMENT

- DEVELOP LONG-TERM (TO POST-2000 ERA) R&D PLANS (BOTH TECHNOLOGY-LIMITED AND RESOURCE-CONSTRAINED) TO DEVELOP TECHNOLOGIES REQUIRED FOR DEFENSE OF THE U.S. AND ITS ALLIES AGAINST BALLISTIC MISSILES

- FY 84 AND FY 85 PROGRAM RECOMMENDATIONS DUE TO NSC BY 15 JUNE 1983

- LONG-TERM PLAN DUE TO PRESIDENT 1 OCTOBER 1983

6-28-83-9

Figure 7.

want any of these, Mr. President? Instead, the briefing delivered by Mr. Gardner emphasized that a high level of 99.975 efficiency is the standard for evaluation. Perhaps this is a reasonable requirement to place on a system of strategic defenses before we go ahead. The point is, it is a strategic requirement—not a technological one. Establishing how effective a system has to be in order to be useful is a function for national leaders to perform. And it's a function they can only perform effectively if they are served by experts who have no need to inject political considerations into scientific analysis. *The San Diego Union* made the point effectively in a July 1983 editorial:

"Mr. Gardner's argument, and the argument of many critics of strategic defense, is that most of the quick-to-deploy systems would knock out 'only' 95 to 99 percent of a Soviet attack. In other words, they would save 50 million to 150 million lives, but that's not good enough for a nuclear war.

"That may or may not be valid strategy. Nuclear physicist Edward Teller argues, convincingly, that a fast, crude, but cheap defense system is precisely what's needed. Early defenses would immediately close the vulnerability of U.S. missiles . . . and would [work out] some of the technological kinks that any defense system will face—like how to defend our defensive satellites against attack themselves. Then, when more exotic technology comes along, we'll be ready.

"Valid or not, all these strategic points are, well, strategic—not technological."

This was all tragically predictable. Two previous presidents, Eisenhower and Kennedy, each toyed with the idea of a strategic defense. Each saw his idea perish in the bowels of the McNamara defense department. Whether Ronald Reagan eventually learns that lesson, and renews his call with stricter instructions or more independent investigators, is probably the key to future strategic defense. It is unlikely that a proposal will ever bubble up out of the military.

The lesson to be gleaned from the Pentagon's strategic defense study, and from most of military history, is clear: To cut down on waste and inertia, it is necessary to have some kind of urgent rationale for circumventing usual channels.

This most frequently happens during war. Churchill found enormous amenability to most of his initiatives, within the military, during World War II; there simply was no time to argue. Unfortunately, we cannot afford to wait until the next war to re-think our strategies and re-design our nuclear forces. The next war will be too late.

By the same token needed efforts to trim back the overall procurement morass are likely to run into stiff political opposition unless there is a clear, pressing need to circumvent usual channels. Senators and Representatives will consider a Manhattan-project approach a sneaky attempt to subvert their authority. Pentagon planners will frown at ideas not issuing from their laboratories, not developed through their channels. And, at the same time, any attempt to rebuild America's strength, working through those channels, will fail. Any program to carry America forward into space, or toward a strategic defense, will be plagued with high cost estimates, technological doubters, and congressional cavils.

The obvious solution is to kill two pressing needs with one stone. An American president announces a dramatic new program to defend the frontier of space, scrap the nuclear strategy of MAD, and do it all exclusive of the overwhelming Pentagon bureaucracy. The names of those who took such action in the past echo: Winston Churchill . . . Franklin D. Roosevelt . . . Harry Truman . . . Dwight Eisenhower . . . John F. Kennedy. America needs such leadership now more than ever.

VII

A New Foreign Policy

Everyone knows about the problems, so let us start with the solutions:

– A new institutional and attitudinal arrangement for the Western alliances, centered around a stronger conventional military for Western Europe and Japan.
– New strategic systems emphasizing ground, air, and space-based defenses against nuclear attack.
– A new effort to take the initiative in promoting security, democracy, and development in communist and underdeveloped nations.

These being the solutions, the problems are obvious: America's foreign policy has failed to successfully confront Soviet expansion in Asia, Africa, and Europe. The U.S. has won enemies in the Third World by paying great attention to arms and less to development. And it has lost friends in NATO with necessary but frightening talk about "limited nuclear wars," nuclear "warning shots," and "protracted conflict" strategies.

It should also be apparent, though less obvious, that an American commitment to build a strategic defense by the end of this decade would be the country's single greatest foreign policy stroke since the Marshall Plan. The dissolution of America's one-time monopoly on nuclear weapons has undercut the strategic foundation of NATO. The worsening

104

balance of conventional power has forced too great a dependence on nuclear weapons on Western strategists, fanning the fears of Europeans and Americans still further. America's seeming inability to respond to lower-level Soviet aggression undermined its position of leadership with the Third World—in Vietnam, and, perhaps already, Central America. Our reliance on deterrence, to the exclusion of strategic defense, seemed to put our leaders always on the defensive when submitting sensitive arms control proposals before the court of world opinion.

Underlying American foreign policy has been the same enervating strategy that sapped support for our own military at home: Mutual Assured Destruction.

Phil Nikolaides, formerly the deputy director of the Voice of America, now a White House aide and a student of international affairs, compared the role of MAD in foreign policy to the effect you get when you shine a bright flashlight in the eyes of a wild animal at night. The animal freezes. Just so, American foreign policy, hypnotized by the transfixing glare of nuclear holocaust, has behaved like a startled, petrified animal. Almost any policy initiative—using conventional forces in Vietnam or Iran, conducting intelligence gathering or covert action operations in South America, rejecting a proposed treaty for the law of the sea or nuclear missiles in Europe, stepping up America's drive to promote democracy and economic freedom in the Third World, supporting Israel—must be evaluated in terms of the horrifying possibility that anything we do might lead to "increased tensions." And increased tensions might lead to "escalation." And escalation might end in the ultimate escalation. We are all familiar with the chain of mights. What is not so familiar is an American foreign policy without the blinding light in its eyes.

The problems of the Western alliance, which is of paramount importance to our own security, are clear. The rise of neutralism and isolationism. The need to coordinate policy on questions ranging from East-West trade to negotiations in the Middle East. The unfavorable shift in the balance of nuclear and conventional power. It is easy enough to see that if everyone in the U.S. and Europe woke up tomorrow willing to radically increase defense expenditures, confront both real and proxy Soviet aggression in the Third World, restrict cheap credits and technology giveaways to the Soviet economy, and maintain a steely negotiating line at arms control conferences, most of those problems would vanish. There is a pretty solid agreement on ends. But perhaps the main challenge for the West today is to create institutional arrangements that will get us there from here.

Under the subtle but pervasive threat of nuclear violence, Henry Kissinger argues, the alliance is heading toward a "consensus of the fearful," a state of political affairs in which NATO partners take the least action possible, defending their inaction with the observation that every other country is behaving pretty much the same. There is an occasional dramatic setback, like the triumph of the Socialists in Greece, and an occasional NATO revival, like the 1983 elections in West Germany. The trend toward allied inaction, however, continues. Afghanistan and Poland, for all the attention they attracted, scarcely scared up an economic sanction. Jean-Francois Revel put it sardonically in a column for *The Wall Street Journal:* "In my view, the alliance has never been in better shape, and more useful to its members. . . . It provides each ally with a marvelous excuse to remain passive, in front of Soviet expansionism, by blaming its own indecisiveness on other allies' passivity."

Economists such as George Gilder and Jude Wanniski remind us that the real sources of wealth are metaphysical. Economies prosper or fail in accordance with their ability to tap the energy, creativity, and capitalistic courage of producers; the physical world is merely the medium through which those forces operate. A parallel view may apply to the alliance. All the troops and weapons and guarantees in the world were not enough to bind the United States to its ally in Vietnam when the war soured. Can it be that MAD nuclear strategy and no-nuke marchers are undermining our alliance in Europe in the same way limited-conflict schemes and stop-the-war protesters dissolved our support for South Vietnam a decade ago?

Nuclear fear hits Europe with a special vengeance, largely because Europe remains a likely battleground should a U.S.-Soviet crisis ever erupt. It is not that the Europeans are intrinsically selfish, cowardly, or lazy. Rather, Europe's growing uneasiness stems from a rather sensible calculation of the risks and dangers around them. Noted NATO revision advocate Irving Kristol explained the problem to a 1982 conference on "The Atlantic Crisis":

> It seems to me a great mistake to talk about the mood in Europe, the growing neutralism, the growing spirit of appeasement, as if this were something that either erupted arbitrarily from the soul of the public or was created by the agitation of a few intellectuals. The mood of appeasement and neutralism in Europe is a perfectly rational response to the military structure and military strategy of NATO. Unless the structure and strategy are radically revised, that mood can only become stronger and will, in the end, triumph.
>
> You cannot ask a people to stick with a military strategy and military posture which insures that in case of conflict they will not survive. That is the European situation. In the 1950s, in an act of supreme idiocy, we decided to base their defense on nuclear weapons. Since then, we have been adding more and more weapons, more and more sophisticated weapons, more and more powerful weapons. And suddenly, the Europeans have noticed that Europe is a nuclear battleground. . . .
>
> We must have a policy that offers the European nations a chance to survive a military conflict—if possible a chance to win but at the very least a chance to survive. Any nation faced with nothing better than the prospect of annihilation in a war will become gradually more and more neutralist, more and more ready to appease.

An American defense that defends is the obvious way to meet that need. A U.S. strategic defense in space would protect not just our cities, but the cities of Western Europe, from a nuclear strike. Indeed, the Europeans might be encouraged to share the costs of our defense and to emulate other measures—civil defense, bomber defenses, and so on. (Many European countries, as we have noted, have civil defenses much more extensive than ours. They have never felt defended by MAD to begin with.)

The old strategic formula of MAD left the United States with a pair of unattractive options in Europe. One, to accept the current trends but hope to continue to prop up the alliance with liturgical calls for unity and appeals to the good of all. That policy did not work throughout the 1970s, because it was aimed at convincing Europeans to eschew their own self-interest in order to pursue some lofty and intangible greater purpose. "Even if we do nothing," Kissinger argues, "we will see important changes in five years. . . . I would like to see these changes made in a constructive rather than a destructive direction." Europe's fears, precisely because they are not unwarranted, cannot be removed through better public relations.

Option two is to attempt to shock Europe into action; the shocker most generally offered is a phased withdrawal of American troops from the continent. There are some good arguments for this position. Though Europe continues to bear the largest share of the burden of defending Europe, there is valid argument to be made that its share, considering its economic strength and population, ought to be 100 percent, not the 40 to 60 percent variously estimated now. And even talk of withdrawal can help to clarify the purpose of the alliance: Why must Americans beg Europeans to allow American troops to defend them? "The knowledge that a man is to be hanged in a fortnight," Samuel Johnson once said, "concentrates the mind wonderfully."

Strategic defense would enhance either approach—a continued American presence in Europe, or a conventional withdrawal. It expands our influence by guaranteeing security for ourselves and for our allies. At the same time, it opens up a whole range of options previously foreclosed by the psychology of MAD. It is doubtful, when Dean Acheson and George Kennan were designing America's postwar foreign policy, that they thought the Soviet Union, with its weak economy and internal unrest, would continue to be a threat to the United States. NATO was a provisional strategy for containing Soviet ambitions in Europe. But as political scientist David Sidorsky notes, "The Soviets succeeded in countering containment by leapfrogging over it and by fostering aggression at the [edge] of their empire in Korea and Vietnam. In 1954 in the arms deal with Egypt . . . Syria . . . Cuba . . . North Vietnam . . . and so forth, the Soviets forced the United States to contain on such a variety of fronts that a purely defensive strategy became questionable." Like the animal frozen by the flashlight, the U.S. was unable to respond, leaving Soviet foreign policy free to maneuver at will around the periphery. "Now if we cannot have a high-risk or rollback policy in a nuclear age . . . and if we cannot (as was shown in the case of Poland) have a highly ideological policy of confrontation, what policy can we have as an Atlantic Alliance? What would make sense: to strengthen containment, or restore detente, or to look beyond containment and detente?"

Most Americans and Europeans would, of course, prefer to look beyond. They would prefer an active policy that seeks to promote the spread of political and economic freedom— in Eastern Europe, in the Middle East, in the Third World. They would, at the base, like to see an America free to play a positive role, not imposing its own will on other countries, not allowing the Soviets or others to impose their own design, but helping free countries to go where they already want to go.

Deterrence . . . containment . . . detente . . . massive retaliation . . . the buzzwords of past foreign policy suggest their own weaknesses. These political strategies all address the problem of Soviet expansion straightforwardly; they do not address the need for Western expansion. "The lesson of history," writes British historian Hugh Thomas, "is that a society which is not interested in exporting itself—which says, in effect, the Zimbabweans aren't ready for it, or the Brazilians are too many for it—is soon likely to lose confidence in its own values." Just as people need a defense strategy that offers some hope of survival, so they need a political strategy that offers some hope of victory. And, just as MAD now frustrates Western aspirations of conducting such a policy, so a strategy of Assured Survival would serve as a solid bedrock of strength from which to advance it.

"There are only two possibilities in a discussion of the strategic objective," Norman Podhoretz argues in *The Transatlantic Crisis* (New York: The Orwell Press, Committee for a Free World, 1982, ed. Midge Decter). "One is the ideas of 1968–1972, which were that we could create a system of incentives and penalties that would induce the Soviet Union to behave with restraint or moderation in world affairs. The basic assumption was that the Soviet empire was here to stay and that we, ourselves, had a kind of interest in stabilizing it. . . . The alternative strategic objective—what used to be called 'liberation' but which should now more properly be called 'destabilization'—was, in fact, envisaged as the end result of the original policy of containment. . . . That is, we believe the Soviet empire may not turn out to be eternal, and we would support measures that might lead to or encourage its disintegration."

A properly defended Western alliance would be in a position to promote freedom in the East as it has never done before. The Reagan administration has designed an impressive shopping list of tools to carry out such a policy: a beefed up Voice of America and Radio Free Europe program to spread the true story of world events to captive peoples; Project Democracy, aimed at Eastern Europe, but also the developing nations, and seeking to strengthen free institutions as they form; and, in such cases as Poland where the positive program to encourage freedom fails, economic and political sanctions to at least make sure that tyrannical rulers pay the full bill for their own inhumanity. Such proposals have had difficulty, however, winning approval from America's allies. All policy goals in the West have been subordinated to the more pressing need for arms control and cordial relations with the Kremlin. The greatest weakness of our chief adversary, the Soviet Union—the wide rift between its government and its people—has gone unexploited. Detente, with some good reason, has become not just a description of a policy, but a statement of necessity. The danger of conducting a populist foreign policy—one which places the security and the concerns of people, rather than European and Soviet elites, at the center—would be swept away by a Western strategic defense.

So, too, would many of the obstacles to better relations with the Third World. Removing MAD strategy would relieve the U.S. of much of the moral burden it now bears, almost alone, of explaining itself in such forums as the United Nations. Instead, America would be the champion of peace and security. We would offer our protective blanket to all nations that hope to escape the horrible consequences of assured destruction. Suddenly, America would be on the moral and diplomatic defensive. Suddenly, too, we would be in a position to offer the developing nations the kind of economic partnership they have long sought: building a bridge into space. An enlightened foreign policy would encourage the developing nations to share in the exploration and exploitation of space—renting space in the shuttle for use by Third World governments and businesses, helping to establish joint ventures between Third World businesses and American industry, leasing or selling U.S. satellites and other technology.

The potential of solar energy generation from space would make available vast amounts of cheap, clean power desperately sought by the developing nations. These countries, as well as our own trading partners in the industrial world, have already shown great interest in such projects. Studies of the solar power satellite concept are underway in Canada, Great Britain, France, Germany, Japan, and the Soviet Union. The governments of Austria, India, Nigeria, and other countries are helping their own industries keep track of the progress made on such projects. In 1980, the Japanese government conducted a thorough study of the implications of American space development for Japanese industry and society. The report concluded: "The world is in a major transitional stage to enter the space utilization and Japan, too, should ride the wave of the future and move steadily forward—it is necessary to plan for Japan's development of the space industry in line with the U.S. and Europe from the standpoint of a long range view and global outlook."

Nuclear security for our allies, conventional security backed by renewed American will, and economic expansion: These are the cornerstones of a new foreign policy founded on strategic defense. Together, they form a policy along much the same lines as Lenin's famous call for "Bread, Peace, and Land." Once again, America's own example would become an unabashed model for emulation by others. America's influence would be something to be desired and expanded; American power, something to be used: American growth, a vehicle for world prosperity.

VIII

Answering the Critics

Almost everyone is attracted to the idea of a defense against nuclear terror. Hawks and doves alike can unite behind the principle of stepping away from the MAD strategy of mutual horror. Still, the breadth of actions that must be taken to achieve a new strategy of survival, and the sheer audacity of the undertaking, are bound to raise a number of concerns—some of them legitimate reservations or aguments, some of them disingenuous cavils generated by those who, at the base, would prefer to see the United States remain without a defense.

Much of the opposition to strategic defense is not active opposition at all, but simple inertia. Criticisms are of the yes-but-what-if variety: yes, but what if the Soviets do this; yes, but what if our allies do that; yes, but what if the left wheel on the space shuttle explodes as it places the one-hundred-and-forty-ninth satellite into position? Most of these arguments are familiar to anyone who remembers the ABM debate of the 1960s and '70s. Most of the arguments stem, in fact, from one of several false premises about defense—premises that were allowed to stand during the last great defense debate, and which, therefore, carried the strategic argument. It is high time for some of them to be shot down.

112

Mutual Assured Destruction has "kept the peace" for 40 years . . .

> —Helen Thomas, United Press International,
> in a White House press conference.

True, in the same sense that it is true that the Treaty of Versailles prevented German expansion for 20 years. If the fallibility of MAD strategy can only be proved by the outbreak of a nuclear war, then let us pray never to receive the decisive evidence.

The argument we offer against MAD is not that it has already caused a nuclear war; obviously, it has not. It is that MAD strategy is *likely* to cause one at some point in the future. Comparing the evolution of American strength and American foreign policy under MAD to what would likely be its evolution under Assured Survival, we can reasonably project that strategic defense would be more likely to prevent all-out war—with the added, crucial advantage that if it does not, we are not totally without defense.

One other point about the "MAD has kept the peace" argument: It hasn't. MAD has, at least so far, kept us out of an all-out nuclear war. It has not, on any other level, eliminated conflict. Nuclear weapons do not keep the Soviet Union from conducting a policy of terror and violence from Afghanistan to Poland, the Middle East, and Central America. Nuclear weapons do keep the West from responding. We cannot even say truthfully that MAD strategy has prevented nuclear weapons from being used. As Michael Novak, the well-known author and religion commentator, noted in *National Review,* "such weapons have two quite different uses. The most obvious use is through their explosion in warfare. The more subtle use is through intimidation, since powers that possess them exercise over others that do not a threat beside which conventional armed forces pale."

The Soviet Union has proved deft at delivering such threats and manipulating Western fears. Only in the narrowest, most superficial sense can we say that Mutual Assured Destruction has "kept the peace."

All our expensive equipment can be blown out of space
"by a single nuclear explosion."
> —William Broad, editor, *Science Magazine*,
> in a *New York Times* column.

The Soviets, in other words, would set off a single nuclear explosion in space which would emit an electromagnetic pulse that would wipe out our most sensitive electronic hardware. Broad, of course, is absolutely right to raise this possibility, since existing U.S. satellites are vulnerable to just such an attack. (So, of course, are most of the Soviet satellites, which would also be hit.) Unfortunately, Broad's thesis, thanks to some misleading headlines in the *Times,* was widely misconstrued as applying to all possible satellites, including anti-missile defenses. It has no relevant connection to these whatsoever.

In fact, reducing the vulnerability of American assets in space is one of the chief aims of defense-in-space advocates. Satellites can be hardened, and electronic equipment redesigned and shielded, to protect against a single-explosion attack. The Pentagon is already fast at work on this, and is also seeking to achieve "redundancy" for certain key satellite functions—that is, placing in orbit extra satellites that can perform the task of vital hardware should it be knocked out.

> *"Whatever exotic technology we finally settle on, we must believe that, like every other weapon system, it will be subject to some countermeasures. . . . If we spend two decades developing, testing and then deploying a system to defeat the Soviet ICBM and SLBM forces, they certainly have ample time to consider, develop, and deploy a variety of countermeasures."*
> —William J. Perry, former Carter defense aide,
> in a *Washington Post* column.

Of course, any system is vulnerable to some countermeasures. And, of course, the Soviet Union will expend a great deal of energy to maintain the potency of its offensive threat. For our part, the U.S. will seek counter-countermeasures. This is called competition.

The first question is, who is likely to excel at a rapid-paced, high-technology race for superior tactics? Common sense, and recent evidence from the Falklands and the Middle East, suggest it will be the United States. This will hold even more true if the U.S. decides not to spend "two decades developing, testing, and deploying a system to defeat Soviet ICBM and SLBM forces." If, instead, we move strategic systems onto a fast-track, high-priority model the Soviets will have two or three years, not decades, to respond to our latest defense. And, as they begin to devise countermeasures and build the hardware to perform them, we will already be deploying the next round of strategic defenses—high energy lasers, particle beam weapons, and so on. Meanwhile, look what has happened: The United States, instead of trying to match the Soviets missile for missile in a tedious, production-based race, has diverted vast resources from the Kremlin's offensive buildup. Every ruble that is spent trying to counter American defenses is a ruble that could have been spent building more missiles, or sending more Soviet agents to Central America.

These overall points must be kept in mind as we evaluate the threat that particular Soviet countermeasures could pose for a new American strategy of defense. Even so, it is worth considering several possible countermeasures individually.

Deception: The Soviets might deploy unarmed missiles, or develop electronic spoofing or jamming methods, in an attempt to confuse American defenses in space into firing at non-nuclear targets. If this deception involved firing phoney missiles, it is a losing strategy: Simulating the lift of a nuclear missile by using a non-armed vehicle would cost nearly as much as simply building another missile. If a first-generation U.S. defense in space employs simple, non-laser technology, we would be in a position to simply add new satellites to the system as we saw the Soviets constructing decoys. In the case of both decoying and jamming, it would be very difficult to guarantee that all of the several satellites within range of a particular missile site could be fooled. So the decoyer's advantage is more complicated than it sounds. Finally, guidance and tracking technology is one area in which U.S. conventional weapons typically excel. Israeli pilots flying American jets over Syria during the 1982 occupation of

Lebanon were able to overcome deception tactics with ease. It is not unreasonable to expect that our space systems would be able to do the same.

Conventional attack: A second possible means of defeating an American strategic defense is to knock it out of the sky with conventional anti-satellite weapons. The Soviets, as we have said, have already developed and tested such weapons in recent years and, by all accounts, are now relatively skilled at using them.

Any conventional attack scenario, however, must start from the realization that it would take more than 48 hours for the Soviets to target and shoot down a large fleet of missile defense satellites as they travel over the Soviet Union. The Kremlin could hardly expect an American president to stand by and watch America's defenses shot out of the sky. More likely, he would warn the Soviets to stop and, if they continued, take action against the source of the anti-satellite attacks. The complications and sheer time delays imposed by a large fleet of low-technology satellites—as against a gold-plated, small fleet of expensive laser satellites—are another argument in favor of deploying a first generation space defense now.

And, just as satellites can be attacked, so can the vehicles that attack the satellites. An airborne defense satellite would be able to shoot down not just nuclear missiles, but anti-satellite weapons as well. Decoy satellites, and decoy electronics, could also be used to divert anti-satellite weapons from their targets. Ground-based lasers could aim at, and knock out, the attack missiles as well. The technology and cost of building ground-based lasers simply to divert anti-satellite weapons from their course will become available much sooner than the more advanced technology needed to use lasers as an anti-missile defense.

Laser attack: Since Soviet investment in lasers has been five times that of the U.S. in comparable dollars, and since that investment appears to have bought the Soviets a significant lead in many laser applications, it is important to consider the prospect of a Soviet ground-based laser attacking U.S. defense satellites. As a means of attacking the entire defense system, lasers would face the same time delays and uncertainties as a full-scale attack using conventional anti-satellite vehicles. Lasers would also be vulnerable to some of the same decoying and evasion devices used against simpler attack methods. They would, in addition, be susceptible to mirror reflectors, special deflection paints and coatings, and other laser "hardening" measures.

Finally, all three of the propounded Soviet countermeasures—deception, conventional attack, and laser attack—would have to deal with the prospect of U.S. "reinforcements," anti-missile satellites held in reserve to replace satellites put out of commission by a Soviet attack.

Measures; countermeasures; counter-countermeasures; counter-counter-countermeasures. All four terms, believe it or not, are to be found in various discussions of the problems of space warfare. Ultimately, Perry's countermeasure argument answers itself: "We must believe that, like every other weapon system, it will be subject to some countermeasures." No strategy or system is invulnerable. The question remains, Who is likely to win a high-technology, counter-for-counter race? And, beyond this, even if the Soviets should gain a decisive edge, would their advantage ever be decisive enough to convince them they could defeat our defense system and succeed in a first-strike attack?

> *A strategic defense is "decades away."*
> —*The New Republic*, April 1983.

On the contrary, strategic defenses have already been designed that could be built starting tomorrow. Provided, that is, that America make a commitment, starting now, to use available technology for a first generation defense, and to let laser beam and microwave breakthroughs come when they will. Technology skeptics are urged to consult any of four sources:

1. Industry evaluations by such private firms as Boeing and United Technologies. Analysts considering the idea of non-laser technologies for space-based defense said they saw no technological obstacles.
2. Congressional testimony by Pentagon researcher Dr.

John Gardner. Gardner—backed by other Pentagon officials such as Defense research head Richard De-Lauer—said proposals for simple-technology strategic defenses have been examined and are "technologically sound." The sole remaining doubts in the military's thinking, apparently, have to do with politics (will the White House and Congress lead the way?) and priorities (can defenses be built quickly and, thus, efficiently?).

3. Project Defender. Project Defender was the result of a study launched in 1958 to consider the possibility of building anti-ballistic missile defenses in space. Project Defender documents, released late in 1982, reveal a consensus among experts on the project that such a defense could be built within five to six years at a reasonable cost. (See Appendix D)

4. The Soviet Union. A 1978 CIA study concludes that Soviet defenses already completed might limit Russian casualties to 15–20 million in an all-out nuclear war. (Thirty million Russians died in World War II alone.) And this level of security was achieved without the most effective system of all: an anti-missile defense in space.

Still, a strategic defense would cost "between $200 million and $300 billion. . . . Once we begin to talk about other more exotic concepts, that price tag will continue to increase."
—Senator Larry Pressler, Congressional Record.

Pressler's estimate, which has been widely circulated, relies largely on estimates of more than $150 billion for laser and particle beam weapons. Such weapons might, indeed, cost that much—which is why most advocates of a true defense call for simpler, available systems.

A similar, but more realistic estimate of $50 billion for strategic defense has been issued by the Pentagon. Its estimate for a series of strategic defenses—anti-ballistic defense in space, point defenses and air defense on the ground, and passive civil defense for our citizens—is closer to reality. The Pentagon bases that $50 billion estimate, however, on a ten-year-plus building cycle. In other words, the Pentagon's estimates, like Pressler's even wilder estimates for laser systems, are based on building strategic defenses the same way we now build tanks, ships, and planes: through the unwieldy procurement process that governs regular channels.

In that sense, his estimate is accurate. But it is not an estimate of what a defense *must* cost—only of what it will cost, if we build it through the bureaucracy. The American people, and their leaders, need not decide on that approach at all. They might decide that a defense against nuclear weapons is high priority, to be built using the same procedures we used on other high priority military needs, such as the atom bomb, the ICBM, the moon landing. In that case, a strategic defense system would cost $15 to $20 billion.

Even so, suppose the Pentagon is right, and a viable American strategic defense would cost $50 billion, that is, about one-fifth of the military budget for a single year. With the system will go all the economic and geopolitical advantages of American superiority in space. Hence, even if the high estimates by defense opponents are correct, defense might still be a bargain. Super-hardening of 100 MX missile silos will cost $10 to $20 billion alone; building Jimmy Carter's race-track scheme was estimated to cost $30 to $60 billion. Can we afford not to try a different approach to the arms race?

An American defense would constitute "a direct violation of the Soviet-American ABM agreement and protocols."
—Soviet News Agency, TASS.

In the short run, the 1972 anti-ballistic missile treaty prohibits little. Point defenses can be constructed around the MX and other missiles. Research and development on other systems can continue. And, even in the long haul, the United States can, if it chooses, treat the treaty Soviet-style, using loopholes in the definition of what an ABM system is.

The better approach is to exercise our option—explicitly stated in the treaty—to give the Soviets six months warning and then withdraw from the pact altogether. If, in fact, defense is a good thing, then the ABM treaty is a bad one. Not just for the U.S., but for both sides. The day an American president renounces the pact—which, incidentally, the Soviets routinely violate—he could invite the Kremlin to join us in the transition from a world of Mutual Assured Destruction to one of Assured Survival. Treaties are a means, not an end in themselves. If the ABM treaty must be torn up in order to rid the world of the threat of nuclear holocaust, then let's start tearing.

An American defense would be so perfect it would encourage a "panicky reaction" from the Soviet Union, flirting with the possibility of a nuclear war.
                                    —Editorial, *The New York Times.*

Indeed, if a defense were perfect, the question is, what would the Soviets do about it? Launch a first strike on the U.S.? Not likely, if, in fact, our nuclear deterrent is as sound as alleged. More probable, the Soviets would rapidly proceed to develop their own, similar system. Critics have an answer for this, too, arguing that it would simply "fuel the arms race."

The apocalyptic scenarios always assume a Soviet Union suddenly faced with a U.S. ready to achieve a perfect defense tomorrow. In fact, the Kremlin would be making a series of marginal choices; and at each point along the decision curve, it would remain as irrational for the Soviets to attack the U.S. as it is now. Would the Soviets attack as we complete our ground-based defense? Of course not; no fundamental change in the balance of power is threatened. As we put up our first satellite? No; and so on down the line. The stronger U.S. defenses become, the less sense a Soviet strike makes— but the process is marginal, not an all-for-one shot.

Perhaps the soundest refutation of the argument that the Soviets would panic came from nuclear physicist Edward Teller: "If we have a defensive advantage, the Soviets can be sure that this is no real danger to them. They know we are not going to use it; we are not going to start a nuclear war. . . . We need a good defense, and a good defense of necessity is preceded by a marginal defense and later by a better defense."

*A United States defense would be so imperfect "we would still
be reliant" on offensive weapons and MAD strategy.*
           —Anthony Lewis, *New York Times* column.

This is the ironic flip side to the previous argument. In
essence, it means that until someone devises a system so perfect that it is guaranteed to knock down every missile,
bomber, and other delivery vehicle, and defeat every
possible countermeasure, we cannot start down the road to
defense.

In fact, there will never be a perfect defense, not against
the bullet, against the tank, against nuclear weapons. What
can be done is to complicate an attacker's calculations, blunt
his forces, and save millions of lives. The important distinction to make here is between *deterrence* and *MAD strategy*, a
special case of deterrence. MAD tells us that the key to peace
and security is an assured capability by each side to reduce
the other to rubble. The obvious emphasis is on offense;
saving 30 million Americans is less critical than blowing up
30 million Russians. Deterrence, on the other hand, recognizes that you can persuade an attacker not to attack by
showing him his attack won't work. And if his attack won't
work, then it's obvious he can't destroy you, and you do not,
therefore, have a MAD situation.

Building strategic defenses would fuel an "arms race in space."
           —Harold Brown, former Secretary of Defense,
           Washington Post column.

That is one way of putting it. Still, if space can enable us to
remove the threat of nuclear annihilation, why not an "arms
race in space"? Wouldn't it be better for the U.S. and Soviets
to compete in building defensive systems and counter-
countermeasures than to continue on their present offen-
sive-only track? If the final shootout is ever to come, let it
come above our heads and not at them. The shift to defense
will not end U.S.-Soviet competition and no one claims it will;
it will, however, shift that competition to a different ground
that is likely to be more stable and, incidentally, favor the
U.S.

Furthermore, the idea that a strategic defense would create a race for space that would otherwise not occur is absurd. The Soviets have already threatened the right of free access to space by deploying and testing anti-satellite weaponry—despite repeated U.S. offers to sign a treaty banning such weapons, and a unilateral U.S. decision not to deploy them. The United States can either defend the frontier or withdraw.

Money for a true defense will come from the budgets of "more urgent needs," such as the MX missile, B-1 bomber, conventional forces, etc.
    —Retired Admiral Elmo Zumwalt,
    former Chief of Naval Operations,
    The Wall Street Journal editorial page.

Any worthwhile program might come at the expense of another. Perhaps we should not build the MX, because it threatens the B-1. Perhaps we should not build the B-1, because it threatens our troop levels in Europe? And so on down the line.

In fact, almost every strategic weapons system to be built in the next five years faces grave funding problems. The urgent need is to come up with a military rebuilding program that can sustain public support for a number of years. A defense that defends is that program. The renewed public support for the military in general that will flow from a crash effort to build a true defense will, far from eliminating other weapons, help them win approval as well.

Money for defense in space will have to come from funds for peaceful development of space—space "will be militarized."
    —Senator Pressler, in the *Christian Science Monitor.*

In fact, like the alleged tradeoff between defense and offense within the military, the choice between peace and war in space is largely a false choice. Development of space will produce both military and economic benefits. One of the greatest barriers to faster development has been the artificial separation of "military" and "peaceful" objectives. Instead, goals and strategies should be merged as much as possible. A core technology approach, seeking to reduce transport costs, achieve further advances in miniaturization of components, and enhance the survivability of all systems in space, is the answer both to our strategic weakness and economic under-development in space.

IX

The End of Something

Some say the world will end in fire. Others say it can dance above the pit indefinitely along the Mutual Assured Destruction tightrope.

Most of human history teaches us that weapons, once built, will be used. On the simple face of it, then, we ought to be preparing for the possibility that nuclear weapons will again be fired. Because the world has accepted for so many years the logic of nuclear terror, we have grown accustomed to thinking largely in terms of short-term imperatives: getting the next weapon approved by Congress, signing another arms control treaty with the Soviets, defusing the latest set of no-nuke rallies in Europe. In the political struggle to determine the next step, we have lost sight of where we hope our next steps will take us. We have compared strategies as if they involved only the next few steps down the pavement. In fact, the different strategies for nuclear survival are each a long and complicated road. We ought to think about where those roads can reasonably be expected to end. There are only three possibilities.

One possible end is international nuclear disarmament. The United States, the Soviet Union, and the rest of the countries armed with nuclear weapons might jointly agree to scrap those weapons and put an end to the offensive threat simply by dismantling their offenses.

124

Putting the genie back in the bottle would be difficult, but it has been done (infrequently) before. The world has managed to prevent, so far, large scale use of chemical weaponry on civilian populations. It is perhaps a wonder of World War II that Hitler did not manage to contaminate a London or Paris—or Chicago—with a deadly agent placed in the population's water supply. Even such limited successes, however, seldom involved the destruction of an entire class of weapons.

Furthermore, we might legitimately wonder about the prospect that all the nuclear powers will be willing to lay down their weapons, either at once or through a series of programmed steps. Anything less than total nuclear disarmament by other countries is likely to prevent the U.S. and the Soviets from dismantling their own forces. It only takes one country to thwart such an agreement, for no one would want any one country to enjoy the luxury of nuclear monopoly.

More fundamentally, can we be sure that the nuclear powers would want to disarm, even if they could agree to do so jointly? In their relations with one another, it is true, the nuclear powers must act with restraint; their options in the conduct of foreign policy are more limited than they would be without such weapons. But in dealing with non-nuclear powers—most of the world—these superpowers enjoy a decisive advantage. They have a button; the others do not.

Let us assume, finally, that all the nuclear nations agree to disarm; that all the details—including, for example, what happens to the tactical nuclear weapons on which NATO relies for its conventional defense—can be worked out. What would happen if one side cheated, and held out a reserve of 250 easily hidden bombs? That cheater would become the sole nuclear power and could impose its will on the rest of the world for as long as it maintained its own will to do so. Suppose, even, that no one cheated and all nuclear weapons were abolished. What would prevent an aggressive leader from someday building a small reserve and, again, mastering the world—reopening Pandora's box?

There may, indeed, be a future without nuclear weapons. We cannot, however, un-invent the technology and know-

how that built them. "You cannot," as former Defense
official William Perry wrote in *The Washington Post*, "repeal
$E = MC^2$." Even a totally disarmed world would face the constant threat of nuclear destruction, would have to maintain
incredible safeguards to make sure that the right materials
never fell into the wrong hands.

The second possible end for mankind is perpetual nuclear
stalemate under a combination of offensive arms buildups
and diplomatic arms control or reduction agreements. It is
important to note that the course of arms control *per se* does
not equal the course of disarmament. President Ronald
Reagan explained what has long gone unexplained about
arms control in his address to the nation in March 1983: "If
the Soviet Union will join with us in our effort to achieve
major arms reduction we will have succeeded in stabilizing
the nuclear balance. Nevertheless, it will still be necessary to
rely on the specter of retaliation—on mutual threat, and that
is a sad commentary on the human condition."

It is argued, of course, that a series of arms limitations
might form a psychology of confidence that could in turn
make disarmament possible. The history of recent arms control agreements seems to suggest just the opposite—Soviet
treaty violations of the terms of the chemical weapons convention, Helsinki, ABM, and SALT I and II, have proved a
major stumbling block to future arms control by undermining the degree of trust required to make the process succeed.

Still, we can hope. As we consider the course of arms control *per se*, however, let us remember that it is only that—
arms control, not arms elimination. It involves indefinite
extensions of the doctrine of Mutual Assured Destruction.
Arms control ceases to be an inextricable ally of MAD only at
the point that it becomes disarmament—which is, as we have
said, a separate matter. Even as a separate matter, arms control agreements can perform a vital function by helping to
ensure that each side maintain its assured second-strike capability to destroy the other. That is what the United States and
the Soviet Union sought to do in 1972 when they expressly
foreclosed their option, for the time being, to defend against
each other's nuclear arsenal. Let us at least recognize,
though, that arms control in and of itself is an attempt to

stabilize and prolong the threat of nuclear destruction—not eliminate it.

Can this strategy be sustained until the utopian solution of disarmament comes along? Probably not. Just consider all the things that must happen in order for MAD doctrine to produce a stable, long-term peace.

For MAD to do its job of deterring conflict even in the short term, the MAD vision must be shared by both sides. It does no good to have the "correct" understanding of nuclear warfare if your opponent does not share it. Yet all the evidence seems to indicate that the Soviets do not share the American view of nuclear strategy. Soviet military journals ridicule the MAD tenet that nuclear war is unwinnable and stress that with solid preparation, including defense of one's own population, the attacking country can inflict massive damage without being greatly damaged itself.

In fact, MAD does not foreclose the possibility of one side launching and winning a nuclear war. For assured destruction to deter war, it must be *mutual* assured destruction. If one side can compile a sufficient stockpile of offensive weapons, and develop a workable system of defense, it may hope to (A) launch a knockout punch that will destroy the other side's retaliatory forces and (B) largely absorb any surviving forces without sustaining unacceptable damage. Given the history of Russia, and the character of the Soviet government, the Kremlin's version of "unacceptable damage" is undoubtedly different from ours. As Harvard historian Richard Pipes wrote: "A country that since 1914 has lost, as a result of two world wars, a civil war, famine, and various 'purges,' [and] perhaps up to 60 million citizens, must define 'unacceptable damage' differently from the United States which has known no famine or purges, and whose deaths from all the wars waged since 1775 are estimated at 650,000—fewer casualties than Russia suffered in the 900-day siege of Leningrad in World War II alone."[1]

For MAD to produce peace, then, there is a second important requirement: MAD must not accompany, or indeed produce, radical changes in the balance of power. Yet the

---

[1] Richard Pipes, "Why the Soviet Union thinks it could fight and win a nuclear war," *Commentary*, July 1977.

balance of power, partly as a result of MAD, is shifting toward instability. The moral repulsiveness of retaliation strategies has driven the Western democracies to a state of schizophrenia over military budgets and arms control initiatives. There is growing evidence that such pressures occasionally produce dissent in the Soviet Union, too, but, of course, such protests are small and ineffectual, and the unelected rulers in the Kremlin pay them no more attention than is needed to dispatch a team of KGB agents to break up the dissent groups. The hypnotic effect of MAD nuclear realities, moreover, has weakened the will of the West to respond to lower level threats, out of a pervasive fear that allied action will "increase tensions" that will set off a nuclear war.

For MAD and SALT (or, more recently, START) to keep the nuclear peace, weapons technology must also evolve in directions favorable to its continuation. In recent years, however, the evolution has been just the opposite. As Henry Kissinger outlined in a major article on arms control for *Time* magazine, improvements in guidance technology make even hardened missile silos vulnerable to a first strike. And the MIRVing of missiles—equipping each missile with multiple warheads, each of which can be aimed at a separate target as the missile reenters the atmosphere—has created a frightening drive by each side toward first strike capability. If two powers have 1,000 missiles, each tipped with three warheads for a total of 3,000 warheads each, then either side knows it can target two warheads at each of the other side's missiles—enough to knock the other side's offense off the map—and be left with a reserve of 1,000 nuclear warheads with which to dictate its will. Thus, multiple warheads produce a situation in which each side can knock out the other. This, in turn, creates tremendous pressure to strike first in any crisis. The side that strikes first will win and survive. The side that refrains will perish.

There are grave doubts, then, that the temporary ceasefire imposed by nuclear parity in the late 1960s can go on indefinitely. If the chances are one in 50 that a Cuban missile crisis will lead to nuclear war, then we may be only a few such crises away from the actual event. It will take only one irrational leader one moment of weakness to press a button that is always waiting.

When we look at the actual goals of disarmament, arms control, and MAD—where they want to take us beyond the next two or three steps—the implausibility that these strategies can keep the peace becomes all too clear. The time has come to veer off onto a different path altogether. We will face difficulties traveling that path, just as we face immediate obstacles on our present course. But at least the path of strategic defense ends up in a place we want to be. At least we find that, if we can reach the end, it is an end to be desired. The same can not be said about the ambiguous goals we now seek on the path to Armageddon.

Nothing we do in the short run, of course, will prevent us from continuing to maintain our offensive deterrent, from seeking arms control and even disarmament solutions. The very knowledge that offensive weapons may soon be useless ought to be a powerful incentive for all parties concerned to scrap the nuclear share of the arms race today. At the same time, however, starting down the road to defense will involve radical changes. We will have to proclaim a dramatic new strategy. We will have to pursue it with the same commitment that America made to putting a man on the moon, building a nuclear bomb, carving out the Panama Canal. We will need the support of scientists and politicians, Republicans and Democrats, hawks and doves.

There is a beyond beyond the nuclear age. To reach it, we must build a defense that truly defends.

Appendix A

SOVIET VIOLATIONS OF U.S.-U.S.S.R.
STRATEGIC ARMS AGREEMENTS

Several times in the text, the authors refer to "repeated Soviet violations" of such major accords as the SALT I and II and ABM treaties with the United States.

As the existence of violations is not central to our argument, we have not detailed them within the body of the book. Arms control agreements, we point out, cannot be hurt by the existence of strategic defense, and might be helped. This is the focal point.

Nevertheless, evidence of consistent Soviet cheating on significant strategic pacts does throw into question the degree of reliance some would place on them as a means of keeping the peace. Given that evidence, it would seem that the only sure security for the United States and its allies is a strategy which does not rely on Soviet goodwill to protect our cities.

As we point out in the last chapter, active defense is the only such strategy. It is not necessary to prove that the following violations have actually occurred for a shift to strategic defense to be a good idea. The mere fact that there is controversy over them, however, suggests that we would be wise not to place all our eggs in the SALT basket.

SALT I VIOLATIONS—ABM TREATY

- Soviet SAM testing in ABM mode
- Soviet deployment of ABM Battle Management Radars
- Soviet ABM camouflage
- Soviet falsification of ABM deactivation
- Soviet creation of a new ABM Test Range without prior notification

• Soviet deployment of a rapidly deployable, mobile ABM

SALT I VIOLATIONS—INTERIM AGREEMENT

• Soviet deployment of the heavy SS-19 ICBM as the replacement of the light SS-11 ICBM, which is the most dangerous of all Soviet SALT violations
• Soviet failure to deactivate old ICBMs on time, and falsification of official reports
• Bringing back ICBM equipment to a deactivated ICBM complex
• Keeping 18 SS-9 ICBMs at an ICBM test range, illegally operational
• Soviet deployment of IIIX silos with a configuration too similar to a missile-launch silo
• Soviet massive use of deliberate camouflage concealment, and deception, which actually increased after 1972:

–Encryption of missile telemetry
–Camouflage of ICBM testing, production, deployment
–Concealment of SLBM submarine construction, berthing, dummy subs, berthing tunnels

• Constructing over 68 strategic submarines, when only 62 were allowed; SS-20 IRBM deployment, which should count as ICBM deployment
• Violation of Brezhnev's pledge not to build mobile ICBMs
• Deploying SS-11 ICBMs at SS-4 MRBM sites, probably having a covert soft launch capability
• Keeping about 1,300 to several thousand old ICBMs stockpiled for both covert soft launch and rapid reload of silos for refire

SALT II VIOLATIONS

• Soviet Typhoon SLBM encryption
• Reported Soviet camouflage of new submarines
• SS-18 Mod X ICBM encryption
• SS-NX-19 SLBM encryption
• SS-20 IRBM encryption and deployment
• Continued stockpiling of SS-16 mobile ICBMs
• Soviet AS-3 Kangaroo deployment on Bear bombers

• Soviet AS-6 deployment on Backfire bombers
• Reported Soviet rapid reload/refire exercises for the SS-18 cold-launched ICBMs

OTHER ARMS CONTROL VIOLATIONS

• Over eight Soviet underground nuclear tests probably over 150 kilotrons, in violation of the 1974 Threshold Test Ban Treaty. Several of these high yield underground tests are *unambiguous* violations.
• Over 30 unambiguous Soviet ventings of radioactive debris from underground nuclear tests in violation of the 1963 Limited Test Ban Treaty. These ventings are all *unequivocal*, and resulted in the spread of radioactive debris outside of Soviet borders.
• In addition to the Soviet Combat Brigade deployed in Cuba, Soviet deployment to Cuba since 1970 of Golf and Echo class submarines carrying long-range nuclear missiles, deployment of nuclear-capable MIG-23 fighter bombers to Cuba, deployment of long-range Bear bomber type aircraft capable of carrying nuclear bombs and missiles to Cuba, all in direct violation of the 1962 and 1970 Agreements Prohibiting Offensive Weapons and their support facilities in Cuba. This arms control violation is even more serious than SS-19 deployment.
• The now *confirmed* April 1979 germ warfare accident at Sverdlovsk, indicating conclusive Soviet violation of the 1975 Convention banning germ warfare. Moreover, there is now also conclusive evidence of Soviet use of biological toxins in Southeast and Southwest Asia. The Soviets also have an intercontinental delivery capability for Biological Warfare (BW) weapons. This Soviet arms control treaty violation is easily understandable, and all by itself it has graphically demonstrated the duplicitous Soviet approach to arms control. The Director of Political-Military Affairs of the State Department, Richard Burt, has directly accused the Soviets of violating the 1975 BW Convention.

The source of this list is David S. Sullivan in *The Bitter Fruit of SALT: A Record of Soviet Duplicity* (Houston: Texas Policy Institute, 1982).

Appendix B

TREATY TO LIMIT ABMS AND
AGREEMENT ON OFFENSIVE MISSILES

TREATY ON Abms

The United States of America and the Union of Soviet Socialist Republics, hereinafter referred to as the parties,

PROCEEDING from the premise that nuclear war would have devastating consequences for all mankind,

CONSIDERING that effective measures to limit antiballistic missile systems would be a substantial factor in curbing the race in strategic offensive arms and would lead to a decrease in the risk of outbreak of war involving nuclear weapons,

PROCEEDING from the premise that limitation of antiballistic missile systems, as well as certain agreed measures with respect to limitation of strategic offensive arms, would contribute to the creation of more favorable conditions for further negotiations on limiting strategic arms,

MINDFUL of their obligations under Article VI of the treaty on the nonproliferation of nuclear weapons,

DECLARING their intention to achieve at the earliest possible date the cessation of the nuclear arms race and to take effective measures toward reductions in strategic arms, nuclear disarmament, and general and complete disarmament,

DESIRING to contribute to the relaxation of international tension and the strengthening of trust between states,

HAVE AGREED as follows:

ARTICLE I

(1) Each party undertakes to limit antiballistic missile (ABM)

134

systems and to adopt other measures in accordance with the provisions of this treaty.

(2) Each party undertakes not to deploy ABM systems for a defense of the territory of its country and not to provide a base for such a defense, and not to deploy ABM systems for defense of an individual region except as provided in Article III of this treaty.

ARTICLE II

(1) For the purpose of this treaty an ABM system is a system to counter strategic ballistic missiles or their elements in flight trajectory, currently consisting of:

(A) ABM interceptor missiles, which are interceptor missiles constructed and deployed for an ABM role, or of a type tested in an ABM mode:

(B) ABM launchers, which are launchers constructed and deployed for launching ABM interceptor missiles, and

(C) ABM radars, which are radars constructed and deployed for an ABM role, or of a type tested in an ABM mode.

(2) The ABM system components listed in Paragraph 1 of this article include those which are:

(A) operational,

(B) under construction,

(C) undergoing testing,

(D) undergoing overhaul, repair or conversion or

(E) mothballed.

ARTICLE III

Each party undertakes not to deploy ABM systems or their components except that:

(A) Within one ABM system deployment area having a radius of 150 kilometers and centered on the party's national capital, a party may deploy: (1) No more than 100 ABM launchers and no more than 100 ABM interceptor missiles at launch sites, and (2) ABM radars within no more than six ABM radar complexes, the area of each complex being circular and having a diameter of no more than three kilometers, and

(B) Within one ABM system deployment area having

a radius of 150 kilometers and containing ICBM silo launchers, a party may deploy: (1) No more than 100 ABM launchers and no more than 100 ABM interceptor missiles at launch sites, (2) Two large phased-array ABM radars comparable in potential to corresponding ABM radars operational or under construction on the date of signature of the treaty in an ABM system deployment area containing ICBM silo launchers, and (3) No more than 18 ABM radars each having a potential less than the potential of the smaller of the above-mentioned two large phased-array ABM radars.

ARTICLE IV

The limitations provided for in Article III shall not apply to ABM systems or their components used for development or testing, and located within current or additionally agreed test ranges. Each party may have no more than a total of 15 ABM launchers at test ranges.

ARTICLE V

(1) Each party undertakes not to develop, test or deploy ABM systems or components which are sea-based, air-based or mobile land-based.

(2) Each party undertakes not to develop, test or deploy ABM launchers for launching more than one ABM interceptor missile at a time for each launcher, nor to modify deployed launchers to provide them with a capability, nor to develop, test or deploy automatic or semiautomatic or other similar systems for rapid reload of ABM launchers.

ARTICLE VI

To enhance assurance of the effectiveness of the limitations on ABM systems and their components provided by this treaty, each party undertakes:

(A) Not to give missiles, launchers or radars, other than ABM interceptor missiles, ABM launchers, or ABM radars, capabilities to counter strategic ballistic missiles or their elements in flight trajectory and not to test them in an ABM mode, and

(B) Not to deploy in the future radars for early warning of strategic ballistic missile attack except at locations along the periphery of its national territory and oriented outward.

ARTICLE VII

Subject to the provisions of this treaty, modernization and replacement of ABM systems or their components may be carried out.

ARTICLE VIII

ABM systems or their components in excess of the numbers or outside the area specified in this treaty shall be destroyed or dismantled under agreed procedures within the shortest possible agreed period of time.

ARTICLE IX

To assure the viability and effectiveness of this treaty, each party undertakes not to transfer to other states, and not to deploy outside its national territory, ABM systems or their components limited by this treaty.

ARTICLE X

Each party undertakes not to assume any international obligations which would conflict with this treaty.

ARTICLE XI

The parties undertake to continue active negotiations for limitations on strategic offensive arms.

ARTICLE XII

(1) For the purpose of providing assurance of compliance with the provisions of this treaty, each party shall use a national technical means of verification at its disposal in a manner consistent with generally recognized principles of international law.

(2) Each party undertakes not to interfere with national technical means of verification of the other party operating in accordance with Paragraph 1 of this article.

(3) Each party undertakes not to use deliberate concealment measures which impede verification by national technical means of compliance with the provisions of this treaty. This obligation shall not require changes in current construction, assembly, conversion or overhaul practices.

ARTICLE XIII

(1) To promote the objectives and implementation of the provisions of this treaty, the parties shall establish promptly a standing consultative commission, within the framework of which they will:

(A) Consider questions concerning compliance with the obligations assumed and related situations which may be considered ambiguous;

(B) Provide on a voluntary basis such information as either party considers necessary to assure confidence in compliance with the obligations assumed;

(C) Consider questions involving unintended interference with a national technical means of verification;

(D) Consider possible changes in the strategic situation which have a bearing on the provisions of this treaty;

(E) Agree upon procedures and dates for destruction or dismantling of ABM systems or their components in cases provided for by the provisions of this treaty;

(F) Consider, as appropriate, possible proposals for further increasing the viability of this treaty, including proposals for amendments in accordance with the provisions of this treaty;

(G) Consider, as appropriate, proposals for further measures aimed at limiting strategic arms.

(2) The Parties through consultation shall establish, and may amend as appropriate regulations for the standing consultative commission governing procedures, composition and other relevant matters.

ARTICLE XIV

(1) Each party may propose amendments to this treaty. Agreed amendments shall enter into force in accordance with the procedures governing the entry into force of this treaty.

(2) Five years after entry into force of this treaty, and at five-year intervals thereafter, the parties shall together conduct a review of this treaty.

ARTICLE XV

(1) This treaty shall be of unlimited duration.

(2) Each party shall, in exercising its national sovereignty, have the right to withdraw from this treaty if it decides that extraordinary events related to the subject matter of this treaty have jeopardized its supreme interests. It shall give notice of its decision to the party six months prior to withdrawal from the treaty. Such notice shall include a statement of the extraordinary events the notifying party regards as having jeopardized its supreme interests.

ARTICLE XVI

(1) This treaty shall be subject to ratification in accordance with constitutional procedures of each party. The treaty shall enter into force on the day of the exchange of instruments of ratification.
(2) This treaty shall be registered pursuant to Article 102 of the Charter of the United Nations.

Done in Moscow on May 26, 1972, in two copies, each in the English and Russian languages, both texts being equally authentic.

FOR THE UNITED STATES OF AMERICA
President of the United States of America
FOR THE UNION OF SOVIET SOCIALIST REPUBLICS
General Secretary of the Central Committee of the C.P.S.U.

THE INTERIM AGREEMENT

The Union of Soviet Socialist Republics and the United States of America, hereinafter referred to as the parties,

CONVINCED that the treaty on the limitation of anti-ballistic missile systems and this interim agreement on certain measures with respect to the limitations of strategic offensive arms will contribute to the creation of more favorable conditions for active negotiations on limiting strategic arms as well as to the relaxation of international tension and the strengthening of trust between states,

TAKING into account the relationship between strategic offensive and defensive arms,

MINDFUL of their obligations under Article VI of the treaty on the nonproliferation of nuclear weapons,

HAVE AGREED as follows:

ARTICLE I

The parties undertake not to start construction of additional fixed land-based intercontinental ballistic missile (ICBM) launchers after July 1, 1972.

ARTICLE II

The parties undertake not to convert land-based launchers for light ICBM's, or for ICBM of older types deployed prior to 1964, into land-based launchers for heavy ICBMs of types deployed after that time.

ARTICLE III

The parties undertake to limit submarine-launched ballistic missile (SLBM) launchers and modern ballistic missile submarines to the numbers operational and under construction on the date of signature of this interim agreement, and in addition launchers and submarines constructed under procedures established by the parties as replacements for an equal number of ICBM launchers of older type deployed prior to 1964 or for launchers on older submarines.

ARTICLE IV

Subject to the provisions of this interim agreement, modernization and replacement of strategic offensive ballistic missiles and launchers covered by this interim agreement may be undertaken.

ARTICLE V

(1) For the purpose of providing assurance of compliance with the provisions of this interim agreement, each party shall use national technical means of verification at its disposal in a manner consistent with generally recognized principles of international law.

(2) Each party undertakes not to interfere with the national technical means of verification of the other party in operation in accordance with Paragraph I of this article.

(3) Each party undertakes not to use deliberate concealment measures which impede verification by national technical means of compliance with the provisions of this interim

agreement. This obligation shall not require changes in current construction, assembly, conversion, or overhaul practices.

ARTICLE VI

To promote the objectives and implementation of the provisions of this interim agreement, the parties shall use the standing consultative commission established under Article XIII of the treaty on the limitation of antiballistic missile systems in accordance with the provisions of that article.

ARTICLE VII

The parties undertake to continue active negotiations for limitations on strategic offensive arms. The obligations provided for in this interim agreement shall not prejudice the scope or terms of the limitations on strategic offensive arms which may be worked out in the course of future negotiations.

ARTICLE VIII

(1) This interim agreement shall enter into force upon exchange of written notices of acceptance by each party, which exchange shall take place simultaneously with the exchange of instruments of ratification of the treaty on the limitation of antiballistic missile systems.

(2) This interim agreement shall remain in force for a period of five years unless replaced earlier by an agreement on more complete measures limiting strategic offensive arms. It is the objective of the parties to conduct active follow-up on negotiations with the aim of concluding such an agreement as soon as possible.

(3) Each party shall, in exercising its national sovereignty, have the right to withdraw from this interim agreement if it decides that extraordinary events related to the subject matter of this interim agreement have jeopardized its supreme interests. It shall give notice of its decision to the other party six months prior to withdrawal from this interim agreement. Such notice shall include a statement of the extraordinary events the notifying party regards as having jeopardized its supreme interests.

Done at Moscow on May 26, 1972, in two copies each in the Russian and English languages, both texts being equally authentic.

FOR THE UNION OF SOVIET SOCIALIST REPUBLICS
General Secretary of the Central Committee of the C.P.S.U.
FOR THE UNITED STATES OF AMERICA
The President of the U.S.A.

THE PROTOCOL

The United States of America and the Union of Soviet Socialist Republics, hereinafter referred to as the parties,

Having agreed on certain limitations relating to submarine-launched ballistic missile launchers, and modern ballistic missile submarines, and to replacement procedures, in the interim agreement,

Have agreed as follows:

The parties understand that, under Article III of the interim agreement, for the period during which that agreement remains in force:

The U.S. may have no more than 710 ballistic missile launchers on submarines (SLBMs) and no more than 44 modern ballistic missile submarines. The Soviet Union may have no more than 950 ballistic missile launchers on submarines and no more than 62 modern ballistic missile submarines.

Additional ballistic missile launchers on submarines up to the above-mentioned levels, in the U.S.—over 656 ballistic missile launchers on nuclear powered submarines, operational and under construction, may become operational as replacements for equal numbers of ballistic missile launchers of older types deployed prior to 1964 or of ballistic missile launchers in older submarines.

The deployment of modern SLBMs on any submarine, regardless of type, will be counted against the total level of SLBMs permitted for the U.S. and the U.S.S.R.

This protocol shall be considered an integral part of the interim agreement.

FOR THE UNITED STATES OF AMERICA
The President of the United States of America
FOR THE UNION OF SOVIET SOCIALIST REPUBLICS
The General Secretary of the Central Committee of the C.P.S.U.

Appendix C

PRESIDENT RONALD REAGAN'S REMARKS ON
STRATEGIC DEFENSE, NATIONWIDE TELEVISION ADDRESS
OF MARCH 23, 1983.

THE NUCLEAR THREAT

Now, thus far tonight I have shared with you my thoughts on the problems of national security we must face together. My predecessors in the Oval Office have appeared before you on other occasions to describe the threat posed by Soviet power and have proposed steps to address that threat. But since the advent of nuclear weapons, those steps have been increasingly directed toward the deterrence of aggression through the promise of retaliation. This approach to stability through offensive threat has worked. We and our allies have succeeded in preventing nuclear war for more than three decades. In recent months, however, my advisers, including in particular the Joint Chiefs of Staff, have underscored the necessity to break out of a future that relies solely on offensive retaliation for our security.

Over the course of these discussions, I have become more and more deeply convinced that the human spirit must be capable of rising above dealing with other nations and human beings by threatening their existence. Feeling this way, I believe we must thoroughly examine every opportunity for reducing tensions and for introducing greater stability into the strategic calculus on both sides. One of the most important contributions we can make is, of course, to lower the level of all arms, and particularly nuclear arms. We are engaged right now in several negotiations with the Soviet Union to bring about a mutual reduction of weapons. I will report to you a week from tomorrow my thoughts on that score. But let me just say that I am totally committed to this course.

143

If the Soviet Union will join with us in our effort to achieve major arms reduction we will have succeeded in stabilizing the nuclear balance. Nevertheless it will still be necessary to rely on the specter of retaliation—on mutual threat, and that is a sad commentary on the human condition.

Wouldn't it be better to save lives than to avenge them? Are we not capable of demonstrating our peaceful intentions by applying all our abilities and our ingenuity to achieving a truly lasting stability? I think we are—indeed, we must!

After careful consultation with my advisers, including the Joint Chiefs of Staff, I believe there is a way. Let me share with you a vision of the future which offers hope. It is that we embark on a program to counter the awesome Soviet missile threat with measures that are defensive. Let us turn to the very strengths in technology that spawned our great industrial base and that have given us the quality of life we enjoy today.

What if free people could live secure in the knowledge that their security did not rest upon the threat of instant U.S. retaliation to deter a Soviet attack; that we could intercept and destroy strategic ballistic missiles before they reached our own soil or that of our allies?

I know this is a formidable technical task, one that may not be accomplished before the end of this century. Yet, current technology has attained a level of sophistication where it is reasonable for us to begin this effort. It will take years, probably decades, of effort on many fronts. There will be failures and setbacks just as there will be successes and breakthroughs. And as we proceed we must remain constant in preserving the nuclear deterrent and maintaining a solid capability for flexible response. But isn't it worth every investment necessary to free the world from the threat of nuclear war? We know it is!

In the meantime, we will continue to pursue real reductions in nuclear arms, negotiating from a position of strength that can be insured only by modernizing our strategic forces. At the same time, we must take steps to reduce the risk of conventional military conflict escalating to nuclear war by improving our nonnuclear capabilities. America does possess—now—the technologies to attain very significant improvements in the effectiveness of our conventional, nonnuclear forces. Proceeding boldly with these new technologies, we can significantly reduce any incentive that the Soviet Union may have to threaten attack against the United States or its allies.

HONORING COMMITMENTS

As we pursue our goal of defensive technologies, we recognize that our allies rely upon our strategic offensive power to deter attacks against them. Their vital interests and ours are inextricably linked—their safety and ours are one. And no change in technology can or will alter that reality. We must and shall continue to honor our commitments.

I clearly recognize that defensive systems have limitations and raise certain problems and ambiguities. If paired with offensive systems, they can be viewed as fostering an aggressive policy and no one wants that!

But with these considerations firmly in mind, I call upon the scientific community in our country, those who gave us nuclear weapons, to turn their great talents now to the cause of mankind and world peace: to give us the means of rendering these nuclear weapons impotent and obsolete.

Tonight, consistent with our obligations under the ABM Treaty and recognizing the need for closer consultation with our allies, I am taking an important first step. I am directing a comprehensive and intensive effort to develop a long-term research and development program to begin to achieve our ultimate goal of eliminating the threat posed by strategic nuclear missiles. This could pave the way for arms control measures to eliminate the weapons themselves. We seek neither military superiority nor political advantage. Our only purpose—one all people share—is to search for ways to reduce the danger of nuclear war.

My fellow Americans, tonight we are launching an effort which holds the promise of changing the course of human history. There will be risks, and results take time. But I believe we can do it. As we cross this threshold, I ask for your prayers and support. Thank you, good night and God bless you.

Appendix D

The following is a memo by top defense aide John T. Bosma to Representative Ken Kramer (R. Colo). It is a summary of *Project Defender* (1958—approx. 1964): *space-based ballistic defenses,* undertaken originally by the Advanced Research Project Agency (ARPA) of the Pentagon.

1. Project Defender was a "crash R&D" effort initiated by the Eisenhower administration in 1958 to deal with the then-perceived threat of a massive pre-emptive Soviet ICBM and space attack against the United States. By 1959, this presidentially-mandated effort had resulted in a broad, very-fast-paced effort looking at all phases of BMD, interceptor technologies and configurations, threat and engagement analyses for space-deployed systems, and some remarkable technology development work (specifically, in infrared seekers, prototype kill vehicle guidance and homing "front ends," in warhead designs and target tests using simulated boosters and other targets, and in warhead packaging, with high-altitude tank testing of complete warhead packages to simulate a space environment).

2. The essence of the Project Defender design was *simplicity* and *speed of development.* It was recognized very early on (specifically, around August, 1959) that the strength and affordability of the PD concept was simplicity—and ARPA planners worked hard to keep the concept simple and affordable in the area of space-based (orbital) BMD systems.

3. The project was managed by ARPA, but the Air Force sub-project (BAMBI—Ballistic Missile Boost Intercept) and the Army's Nike Zeus covered the boost-phase and terminal intercept technologies in more detail. However, ARPA also

146

did some remarkable and innovative work in non-nuclear, highly "MIRVed" terminal ABM concepts and technologies by itself, specifically the 50-warhead ARPAT (for ARPA Terminal Defense) system for defending large soft targets, such as SAC bases.

4. The "brain trust" for this highly streamlined, "fast track" R&D project was a group of *20* scientists in the Defense Department. The total project population in mid-1960 was approximately 5,000 people. This project was ARPA's most important effort at that time. By July, 1960, ARPA was spending over $100 million/yr and had 150 contracts out to industry, government laboratories, non-profit research organizations, and universities.

5. It was also recognized early on that the most important go/no-go parameters for a PD deployment involved (1) launch and orbital-support concepts and technologies, and also (2) reliability of components. Regarding the former, it must be stressed that Project Defender involved launching operations of a scale that could best be called "industrial" scale—in fact, the kind of scale originally associated with the 714-mission traffic model NASA originally developed for the space shuttle in the late 1970's. In essence, Project Defender would have required a considerable amount of orbital mass as well as a continuing replacement launch capability. The expected IOC of Defender was 1965–1966, with an anticipated 3-year buildup period. While the original boosters would have been large expendables of the Saturn 1C or Atlas-Centaur variety (with the Saturn 1C taking up 6 6-interceptor satellites at a time), the planners of Project Defender expected to transition to a fully reusable shuttle in the period 1967–1968. This shuttle would have carried 12 of the 6-interceptor "reference" satellites, for a total of 30,000 lbs. placed into low earth orbit, as compared to the 40,000-lb. payload of the expendable boosters of the Saturn 1C variety. However, this reusable shuttle was to have built on the "Space Plane" technologies also being developed (beginning in 1957, under the Air Force) in the *Dyna-Soar* program, which was conceived as a mini-shuttle, as an orbital bomber, and as a surveillance system. Finally, consideration was si-

multaneously being given to a B-70/*Atlas* combination, an approach that would have drawn on the advanced Mach4-5 versions of the B-70 *Valkyrie* bomber then under development by North American Aviation. The B-70 Atlas combination was expected to drop delivery costs to less than $325/lb.

Regarding reliability, the project planners expected to need at least two-order of magnitude improvement in reliability—and also expected to achieve it by the time the full-up system was committed to production in late 1964. The driving emphasis of the project, however, was to use state-of-the-art in electronics and sensors—and above all, to design for strict simplicity in concept and operation. Particularly interesting, given today's attention to C^3 as somehow determining a go/no-go condition for such equivalent projects, was the designer team's insistence on minimizing communications with the ground—even in peacetime, and striving for as much autonomy on the interceptor satellites as possible.

*   *   *

A representative statement from a contract study performed by Convair (which was given the lead role in the SPAD [Space Patrol Active Defense] orbital defense system by ARPA) illustrates the general attitudinal framework within which ARPA and industry planners operated:

> A detailed examination of the SPAD system and components, and a systems study of the optimum orbital, surveillance, interceptor, and other parameters, indicates that the system concept and the design of all the necessary components and functions is feasible for the time period for which the system has been configured (1966 initial deployment). This would require immediate full support of the development program.
> (*Space Patrol Active Defense—Summary*, ZR-AP-037, May, 1960, by Convair/San Diego, p. 3)

It should be noted that this assessment was based on a very considerable amount of analytical, engineering, and laboratory test work conducted by all participants in this project. Full-up warhead deployment tests at simulated altitudes of 175,000 (specifically, a "spinning-spider-web" warhead spanning 50–80 feet, a design now being used for the Army *Hom-*

ing Overlay Experiment, or HOE, ABM experiments in early 1983) were conducted in 1960. Pellet configurations and densities for use with both the spider-web warhead and with a second class of "shotgun cloud" warheads associated with a different class of on-orbit interceptors were tested against simulated Titan I second stages and Atlas sustainer stages and resulted in firm conclusions about pellet materials, densities, and packaging techniques. Moreover, the threat against which Project Defender was oriented was a simultaneous Soviet launch of large numbers of ballistic missiles, the reference threat launches being 500, 1,000 and 2,000 boosters. Even more remarkable was the fact that this project was conducted *before* the United States knew where the Soviets would site their ICBM fields and how densely they would deploy their missiles, factors which were very important to the fundamental PD parameters of orbital altitude, interceptor performance, sensor technology selection, orbital mass, satellite configuration(s), and, above all, *cost.* In essence, this project was conducted amid considerable uncertainty about the most important parameters (specifically, whether the Soviets would "clump" their ICBM launching sites and thereby drive the costs of achieving adequate orbital and interceptor coverage to unaffordable levels) affecting the ultimate cost of Project Defender. Nevertheless, the planners of this project felt they could achieve sufficient performance and reliability to produce an affordable system (roughly set at $22 billion, although the system was never "designed to cost," but rather to an urgent IOC).

The on-orbit elements of Project Defender were also designed around anticipated Soviet countermeasures—particularly "bucket of sand" or "pellet" attacks. Thus, the reference PD satellite featured an armored design and a certain amount of robustness. Indeed, from the beginning of this project, ARPA and industry planners designed their orbital system from the ground up around anticipated Soviet countermeasures, including pellet attacks, infrared decoys, reduced burning times, "clumping" of ICBM launches both geographically and in terms of attack time durations, ground-launched ICBM decoys, and warhead decoys. (The latter class of decoys were viewed as causing considerable economic uncertainty for terminal-ABM systems—and were apparently one factor in an independent ARPA terminal-defense system capable of handling 50 different targets, including undiscriminated heavy decoys—the ARPAT system mentioned earlier.)

*   *   *

Following is a short summary of *Project Defender* technologies and assessments:

... between August 1959 and July 1960, ARPA and DDR&E planners completely reoriented their thinking away from previously preferred in-space nuclear intercept concepts and cast their reference system in terms of a non-nuclear impact-kill interceptor, with miss distances expected to be on the order of 10–30 feet, coming down to 1–2 feet and warhead sizes of 2–11 lbs.

... This reduction in miss distances by two orders of magnitude was done as a result of in-house and contractor studies based on state-of-the-art or anticipated technical developments.

... by July 1960 system tradeoffs had been performed between two extremes: a heavy (58,000-lb.), 140–150 interceptor satellite (including satellite decoys, to convey to a Soviet observer more satellites in orbit than there really were) to a randomly orbiting, high-number (up to 70,000 vehicles) "Random Barrage System" composed of individual tiny kill vehicles. The type and configuration of such satellites was in large measure determined by planning assumptions on whether the Soviets would "clump" their ICBM sites. ARPA planners, however, decided to build on a 6-interceptor "reference" satellite by July 1960 with the full on-orbit mass to be determined by interceptor performances, Soviet ICBM deployment, and other "open" parameters.

... sensor and fire-control problems were viewed as considerable but solvable, particularly with the use of "clever techniques" (a term used frequently by ARPA planners at a July 1960 DDR&E conference on Project Defender). Infrared detectors, signal-to-noise (requiring more background radiation data), and signal processing requirements for the infrared sensors looking at hot-burning ICBM targets were all viewed as solvable or off-the-shelf.

. . . ARPA planners planned to make a final system-design choice and design "freeze" in FY 1962 (indicative of an extremely fast-paced "crash R&D" program). Most Defender contracts ran for one year or less, and frequently there are references in project documents about planning periods involving several *months*. Again, the emphasis was on speed of development and simplicity of design. The full SPAD go-ahead was expected, in mid-1960, to be the first quarter of 1963.

. . . production economies and "learning curves" were a critical factor in Project Defender. The planners realized they were planning on an "industrial scale" for production, launching, and replenishment operations. Production expenditures were expected to start building in 1964, with peaks in 1965–1967.

. . . C^3 and on-orbit computer capabilities were designed around available computer systems (for example, Burroughs computers aboard the reference satellite). However, even in the fire-control systems, planners sought simple computer designs and stressed the need to design for "basic" computer capabilities. C^3 was also viewed as requiring "stripped down" designs—essentially working virtually on IFF (Identification Friend-or-Foe) thresholds. Attack thresholds were expected to be built into the individual interceptor designs.

Conclusion: The attitudinal commitment to conceptual and technical audacity in all elements of Project Defender is one of the most remarkable aspects of the documentation, along with an emphasis on speedy development and design simplicity. The planners conclude that orbital defenses of a high order of competence were effective, affordable, and double *within the state-of-the-art*—a judgment made as early as July 1960. Launching and reliability costs were seen as the most important economic factors, rather than the more technical parameters of detector sensitivity, interceptor performance, etc.

Had such orbital defenses been deployed, using Space-Plane or Dyna-Soar boosters starting in 1967–1968, there is every probability that the United States would have had a fully developed space infrastructure, featuring all of the necessary vehicles and technologies for space operations for industry and science, more than two decades before the space shuttle.

Index